# CRYPTOGRAMS and SPYGRAMS

Norma Gleason

Dover Publications, Inc.
New York

Published in Canada by General Publishing Company, Ltd., 30 Lesmill Road, Don Mills, Toronto, Ontario.
Published in the United Kingdom by Constable and Company, Ltd., 10 Orange Street, London WC2H 7EG.

*Cryptograms and Spygrams* is a new work, first published by Dover Publications, Inc., in 1981.

*International Standard Book Number: 0-486-24036-3*
*Library of Congress Catalog Card Number: 80-68656*

Manufactured in the United States of America
Dover Publications, Inc.
180 Varick Street
New York, N.Y. 10014

# AUTHOR'S NOTE

Seven years ago I could not have imagined that one day I would put together a book of cryptograms and ciphers.

Seven years ago I had never solved a cryptogram. I didn't know a Key Phrase from a door key or a Baconian from a rasher of bacon.

Then it happened. I was feature writer on a weekly newspaper. Looking through the list of associations and societies in an almanac one day I began to notice listings for rather unusual groups: a nudist club, people studying flying saucers, a hopelessly optimistic band advocating the reform of American spelling, a club for fat people who wanted to stay that way and similar organizations.

Thinking it would provide the makings of an interesting feature story, I wrote to the secretaries of some of these groups, asking for information for a contemplated newspaper article. Among those I queried was the American Cryptogram Association. (I couldn't imagine why a national organization would exist solely because of cryptograms. I wondered who they were and what they did.)

Therein was my downfall. I joined the ACA myself and became permanently addicted to cryptograms and ciphers.

Perhaps through this book you too can discover the great fascination and challenge of this kind of puzzle-problem.

As do the writers of most books, I owe thanks to many people who contributed in one way or another. Mike Donner, managing editor of *Games* magazine, coined the delightful name "Spygrams" for my ciphers when they appeared in the magazine, and kindly granted permission for me to use the name in this book.

I also want to thank Will Shortz, associate editor at *Games* and a personal friend, for encouraging me to do this book.

Three expert solvers, all members of the ACA, proof-solved the problems in this book. I owe many thanks to Dr. D. C. B. Marsh, E. E. Alden and William G. Bryan for their painstaking work, suggestions and criticism. They found more errors than I had expected and hopefully all of these have been corrected. Nothing is more irksome to a solver than to have difficulty solving a cryptogram only to learn belatedly that the crypt itself is in error.

I owe special thanks to the American Cryptogram Association for introducing me to this exciting pastime.

To many others too numerous to mention I owe thanks for encouragement, information and suggestions.

To the vice-president and managing editor of Dover Publications, Clarence Strowbridge, thanks for giving me three months off from work on the book in order to make a permanent move from Michigan to Florida.

Lake Helen, Florida
February, 1981

# TO SOLVERS

The puzzles in the first seven chapters of this book are ordinary cryptograms—messages in which one letter of the alphabet is substituted for another, with the substitutions constant throughout any one cipher.

The next seven chapters are ciphers of various types, some used in wartime, some devised for fun—all challenging, all different. Some depend on substitution of letters or symbols for the real letters of the message. Others retain the actual letters but rearrange them so the message appears unreadable to anyone not knowing the key. One cipher masks the message by mixing in extra, unneeded letters.

I have done my best to lay out this book so it will be equally enjoyable for the novice (including those who have shied away from cryptograms because they thought them too difficult), for the somewhat skillful solver and for those more expert. The latter may ignore the clues provided with individual ciphers. In-betweeners may wish to use these clues. Novices will not only require the clues, but may need additional help. This is provided in the Appendix: First Aid for Ailing Solvers. Here you will find help on the ciphers in this book plus solving techniques useful for solving any cryptogram.

Beginners will find it easiest to begin with Chapter I and work their way onward. Other solvers can pick and choose chapters at random.

Good solving!

# CONTENTS

# 1
# THE CAESAR CIPHER (AND VARIATIONS)

"It's difficult to get things started," the Professor remarked to Bruno, "when once we get started, it'll go on all right, you'll see."
*Sylvie and Bruno Concluded*

Julius Caesar may have been a great soldier and conqueror, but when it came to ciphers he was very much the novice.

He invented a simple cipher, which still bears his name, for disguising his messages. The Caesar cipher provides a fine opportunity for novices to become acquainted with letter substitution, the foundation of cryptogrammatic puzzles. Those better acquainted with cryptograms can zip through the problems in this chapter in short order. (But cheer up! You'll find tougher fare in subsequent chapters.)

Caesar's Cipher

*Plain:* A B C D E F G H I J K L M N O P Q R S T U V W X Y Z
*Cipher:* D E F G H I J K L M N O P Q R S T U V W X Y Z A B C

To write VENI, VIDI, VICI, Caesar would find the V in the plaintext alphabet, note the Y shown as the cipher equivalent, and so on. The message would be enciphered YHQL, YLGL, YLFL, a simple shift of three letters all the way through.

Today's version of the Caesar is not limited to a shift of three letters. Rather, it consists of any two alphabets (one plaintext, one cipher) written in normal order, that is, not disarranged or mixed up in any way. To solve a known Caesar cipher, simply "run down the alphabet" (see table) with one of the cipher words until intelligible plaintext results.

For example, given a cipher containing the word ZXBPXO, we would lay it out on paper and write out the next letter of each cipher letter vertically as it normally would follow in the alphabet:

```
Z X B P X O
-----------
A Y C Q Y P   —nothing legible here, so go on:
B Z D R Z Q   —again no plaintext. Go one more and find the
              word.
```

Caesar Alphabets

```
A B C D E F G H I J K L M N O P Q R S T U V W X Y Z
B C D E F G H I J K L M N O P Q R S T U V W X Y Z A
C D E F G H I J K L M N O P Q R S T U V W X Y Z A B
D E F G H I J K L M N O P Q R S T U V W X Y Z A B C
E F G H I J K L M N O P Q R S T U V W X Y Z A B C D
F G H I J K L M N O P Q R S T U V W X Y Z A B C D E
G H I J K L M N O P Q R S T U V W X Y Z A B C D E F
H I J K L M N O P Q R S T U V W X Y Z A B C D E F G
I J K L M N O P Q R S T U V W X Y Z A B C D E F G H
J K L M N O P Q R S T U V W X Y Z A B C D E F G H I
K L M N O P Q R S T U V W X Y Z A B C D E F G H I J
L M N O P Q R S T U V W X Y Z A B C D E F G H I J K
M N O P Q R S T U V W X Y Z A B C D E F G H I J K L
N O P Q R S T U V W X Y Z A B C D E F G H I J K L M
O P Q R S T U V W X Y Z A B C D E F G H I J K L M N
P Q R S T U V W X Y Z A B C D E F G H I J K L M N O
Q R S T U V W X Y Z A B C D E F G H I J K L M N O P
R S T U V W X Y Z A B C D E F G H I J K L M N O P Q
S T U V W X Y Z A B C D E F G H I J K L M N O P Q R
T U V W X Y Z A B C D E F G H I J K L M N O P Q R S
U V W X Y Z A B C D E F G H I J K L M N O P Q R S T
V W X Y Z A B C D E F G H I J K L M N O P Q R S T U
W X Y Z A B C D E F G H I J K L M N O P Q R S T U V
X Y Z A B C D E F G H I J K L M N O P Q R S T U V W
Y Z A B C D E F G H I J K L M N O P Q R S T U V W X
Z A B C D E F G H I J K L M N O P Q R S T U V W X Y
```

To avoid unnecessary tedium, the four Caesar ciphers that follow do not extend beyond four letters backward or seven forward. (In problem No. 1, the first word is hyphenated, the hyphen being represented by an en-dash. All hyphenated words are presented this way in all problems throughout the book.)

## PROBLEMS FOR SOLVING

### 1. There's Got to be One Somewhere!

S G Q D D–P T Z Q S D Q R   N E   N T Q

O N O T K Z S H N M   K H U D   H M   N Q

M D Z Q   B H S H D R;   S G D   N S G D Q

P T Z Q S D Q   H R   N M   S G D

S T Q M O H J D   K N N J H M F   E N Q

S G D   D W H S.

### 2. Aw Shucks, 'Tweren't Nothin'

H J Y Z N O T   D N   O C Z   K M V X O D X Z

J A   R D O C C J G Y D I B   A M J H

J O C Z M   K Z J K G Z   O C Z   C D B C

J K D I D J I   T J P   C V Q Z   J A

T J P M N Z G A.

### 3. Balancing the Budget (asterisk indicates capitalized word)

B H V W H U G D B   L V   D   F D Q F H O O H G

F K H F N;   W R P R U U R Z   L V   D

S U R P L V V R U B   Q R W H;   W R G D B

L V   W K H   R Q O B   F D V K   B R X

K D Y H . . .   V R   V S H Q G

L W   Z L V H O B   *N D B   *O B R Q V

**4. Royal Entombment**

Q E B  Q L J Y  L C  *Q R Q X K H E X J B K,

Q E B  *B D V M Q F X K  H F K D,  T X P

A F P Z L S B O B A  F K  K F K B Q B B K

Q T B K Q V–Q T L  Y V  X K  *B K D I F P E

X O Z E X B L I L D F P Q.

The next four cryptograms are somewhat different. The Caesar cipher is such a simple one that a ten-year-old, knowing the method, could decipher such a message with ease.

A more secure method was devised by Trithemius, a brilliant German-born abbot who, in 1516, wrote the first book on cryptology ever printed.

Trithemius devised the alphabet table shown at the end of this chapter. He enciphered the first letter of a message with the A alphabet, the second letter with the B alphabet and so on.

To compare: the word CODE, in Caesar, could become BNCD (backward shift of one) or any other cipher letters taken from a *single* alphabet row.

Trithemius, however, would use four different alphabet rows to encipher CODE, with the result CPFH, the C being a shift of zero, the P a shift of one (O-P), the F a shift of two (D-EF) and the H a shift of three (E-FGH).

Deciphering a Trithemius with the alphabet table is not difficult, but does tend to become cumbersome.

Accordingly, it is often shortened. Instead of progressing from A all the way to Z, often only three or four alphabets are used, reverting back to the A alphabet. Another variation is to use as many alphabets for each word as there are letters in the word. A three-letter word would use the A, B, C alphabets while a six-letter word would use alphabets A, B, C, D, E and F.

This is a great way to keep a diary as it defies instant analysis by anyone other than an expert.

It's up to you now to find out, by trial and error, or guesswork, which of these Trithemius variations are used in the next three cryptograms.

**5. Think for Yourself**

B P T U S B K K  J A K T Z F  V P L V  F H

P V H R C.

**6. Right in Between**

M P U W  A O A R R J  C B P  D J T H G Y

Y P W  T P  H B R S M S K Z A.  I U  I T

M J F Z E D  B F V Z I J T  T P Q  M V E K

A O F  T P Q  L J V W P J.

**7. Undesirable Verbosity**

P E S E  H  A Q Y C F  D I T I K A H H

D O  B T Z D F F  E C  F  R V V P

K Y E J S G.

(The cryptogram above does not begin with the A alphabet.)

Without departing entirely from the idea of the "alphabet shift," a still more secure way of thwarting unwanted deciphering is by use of a keyword.

Suppose you want to send the message "Meet me at eight by the pool." Pick a keyword, any word at all. Let's say you pick the word CODE. You then write out your message and write the word CODE above it repeatedly, like this:

```
C O D E   C O   D E   C O D E C   O D   E C O
M E E T   M E   A T   E I G H T   B Y   T H E

D E C O
P O O L
```

Then simply encipher your message accordingly, coding the word MEET from the C, O, D and E alphabets respectively, and so on. The word MEET becomes cipher OSHX. This method offers better security since the initial letters of the word do not represent themselves, and since the solver does not know the keyword, it will not be as easy for him to crack the cipher.

The following cryptogram was enciphered with a keyword. The keyword is a five-letter synonym for "scold." All five letters of the keyword come from the first nine letters of the alphabet, ABCDEFGHI. Try to guess the keyword, either by looking up synonyms for "scold" or by anagramming five letters from the nine into a word.

When you have discovered the keyword, write it above the cipher letters repeatedly and then use the alphabet table to decipher the cryptogram. When solving this type of cryptogram, using the table, work backwards. Find the alphabet row first, look along that row for the cipher letter, then to the top of that column for the plaintext letter. Another clue: note one-letter words.

**8. Financial Note**

F L N L R K A Q R R  Q M  I  G M O L:  I

G S N S I U  A K A P  D P N  A P H

X C E M V  X C R M Q  S W A.

# 2
# EASY CRYPTOGRAMS

"Why," said the Dodo, "the best way to explain it is to do it."
*Alice's Adventures in Wonderland*

Did you solve the cryptograms in Chapter 1? Did you think they were too easy? Well, sharpen your pencils! They get harder as you go along (and victory the sweeter)!

It's a big help in solving cryptograms if you know how a cryptogram is constructed. The constructor normally uses two alphabets, one for plaintext, one for the substitute cipher letters. One alphabet, usually the cipher alphabet, is out of order, such as this random mixed example:

*Cipher:* H U D Q Z R K X T B W V O E J A S F N C M Y P I L G
*Plain:* A B C D E F G H I J K L M N O P Q R S T U V W X Y Z

To encode his message, the constructor works from the plaintext to the ciphertext. A's become H's, B's become U's. The solver must do just the opposite. Given ciphertext, he must recover the plaintext.

With any cryptogram, if you get stuck, it's helpful to try to reconstruct the two alphabets. Write out the plaintext alphabet in normal sequence, as above. Better label it "plain" to avoid confusion. Label the blank space above that alphabet "cipher." Then, as you find which cipher letters stand for which plaintext letters, you can start filling in the blank cipher alphabet. This gives you a quick way to see which letters are still unaccounted for, to help you identify the unknown cipher equivalents.

For instance, suppose you have a crypt all solved except one word, which appears as: *cipher*: B W P T
*plain*: U M P

There is only one cipher B in the cryptogram, and you cannot identify for certain its plaintext equivalent. If you write out the alphabet, you may end up with this:

| | | | | | | | | | | | | | | | | | | | | | | | | | | |
|---|---|---|---|---|---|---|---|---|---|---|---|---|---|---|---|---|---|---|---|---|---|---|---|---|---|---|
| *Cipher:* | C | | H | F | N | L | P | M | R | | | E | P | I | S | T | | D | U | O | W | | J | | A | |
| *Plain:* | A | B | C | D | E | F | G | H | I | J | K | L | M | N | O | P | Q | R | S | T | U | V | W | X | Y | Z |

A quick glance at the plaintext alphabet shows that only plain B, J, K, Q, V, X, Z are unaccounted for. Try each in turn for Cipher B. B cannot stand for itself. That leaves JUMP, KUMP, QUMP, VUMP, XUMP and ZUMP. Obviously B = J, making JUMP. Sometimes, of course, the context is clear as to what the word is. But sometimes it is not. With easy cryptograms it is seldom necessary to write out the alphabets. But in dealing with harder cryptograms, the alphabet device will often open up an impasse.

Following are five basic solving techniques which will help you solve any easy to moderately difficult cryptogram.

## FIVE BASIC RULES

**1.** See if there is a one-letter word in the crypt. If there is, it must be A or I, with A most likely. Try writing A under that cipher letter and wherever else that cipher letter appears in the crypt, and see if probable words come to mind. If not, try I.

**2.** A three-letter word is likely to be THE, especially if it starts the crypt or appears more than once.

**3.** Note which cipher letter appears most often. It may represent E. Here is the frequency alphabet:

E T A O N I S R H D L U F C M W P G Y B V K X J Q Z

That is, the letter that appears most often in English writing is E, the second most frequent is T and so on. Of course this does not mean that every cryptogram will contain letters in exactly that order of frequency. But the solver may assume that the cipher letters of highest frequency represent plaintext letters in the first third of the frequency alphabet, while letters that appear less frequently (1 or 2 times) will come from the second half of the frequency alphabet.

**4.** Compare short words with one another. Every two-letter word contains a vowel and a consonant. Try to identify the vowels. Few two-letter words end in A, I or U and few begin with E or Y.

**5.** Look for pattern words—words with repeated letters such as DID, ALL, OFF, TOO, AWAY, EVEN, EVER, and so on. For the novices among us, there are handy lists of pattern words in the Appendix (page 85).

## PROBLEMS FOR SOLVING

### 1. Modern Times

B P M Z O  X S  A F Z H A W F C  F X

O S S K: "X P H  Z F O T  S Y  X P H

P S E A H  M A C ' X  M C.  A P H ' A  F X

P H K  S Y Y M B H  K E C C M C L  P H K

B S W N F C T.  M ' Z Z  L H X  X P H

W F C  S Y  X P H  P S E A H."

(Clues: Compare FX and SX. What could M'ZZ be? You'll find pattern words to match SYYMBH in the Appendix.)

### 2. Magnanimous, What?

F X H F M K  W T  O L X T D F B O  L J

V T L V X T  H N L  E Y K F I D T T

H Y O N  M L A.  O N T M  N F U T  F

D Y I N O  O L  O N T Y D  L H B

D Y E Y P A X L A K  L V Y B Y L B K.

(Clues: One-letter word must be A or I. Compare OL and LJ. If the L is a vowel, which vowel? Pattern words to match VTLVXT are in the Appendix.)

### 3. Oriental Wisdom

*P Y E G Q C Q  J V K M Q V Z:  Y Q  I Y K

F C H C  F  R A Q C B E K G  E C  F

S K K W  S K V  S E M Q  N E G A B Q C.

Y Q  I Y K  L K Q C  G K B  F C H  F

R A Q C B E K G  V Q N F E G C  F  S K K W

S K V Q M Q V.

(Clues: Asterisk denotes a word beginning with a capital letter. Note one-letter word. Check high-frequency letters. Pattern words for SKKW are in the Appendix.)

**4. Ignorance Is Bliss**

R D M  Q Z T  G J C G E R G T M  V Y  G

I N M J Z R  I G N J  Z K  R D G R  L V F

J V E ' R  O E V H  L V F  G N M

Q N V O M,  G R  X M G K R  E V R

F E R Z X  R D M  M E J  V Y  R D M

U V E R D.

(Clues: Lots of easy solving in this one. Note word RDGR. Note the one-letter word. An apostrophe is usually followed by one of two letters. What are the possibilities?)

**5. What About ABC?**

K G Y J M ' V  T N L H Y Z C S  V K J Z K

O L S Y C Z A J Z K C S  F L K N  J S

J Y I J S K J A C.  K N C M  J H Z C J Y M

O S G F  K F G  H C K K C Z V  G B  K N C

J H U N J X C K: K I.

(Clues: Again note the apostrophe. Pattern word for HCKKCZV is in the Appendix.)

**6. Macaroni**

"Q P U C R C U O F L R C L M U I T:

C U I C B L W I G Q T *F D U P I I

*X C C X O I D U X L W I C L W I Y

Q T U ' L," *M O F T T I T *T. *J Y D U L

C U Z I Y I G D Y P I X.

(Clue: Remember, the letter that appears most frequently is usually a substitute for plaintext E.)

**7. Heavy Gas Consumption**

N U D U K O U C N T M O Z T M T F Z T

D U K C L T M L T C T M P F A U C A V

L U A C L? V P I T E T F: C U

G H P Y T F Z P F Y P C ' F E T

M T P Y Z T N E D Y P M.

(Clues: Here's that pattern word FZPF again. Note question mark at end of first sentence. What might that two-letter word be, then, at the beginning of the sentence? Note other clues.)

**8. Cold Country**

*T O W W J P H J C Z Y R X W

P H O T W Y R  Z Y P H J C  Z J  R X W

S F O P C.  U F Y R  F B  Z R  Z Y

Q F I W O W C  S Z R X  Z Q W

R X F M Y H J C Y  F B  B W W R  C W W D.

(Clues: Compare ZY, ZJ, ZR. Is Z a vowel? Which one?)

# 3
# CIPHER-KEYED CRYPTOGRAMS

> He thought he saw a Garden-Door
> That opened with a key;
> He looked again, and found it was
> A Double Rule of Three;
> "And all its mystery," he said,
> "Is clear as day to me!"
>
> *Sylvie and Bruno*

Most newspaper and magazine cryptograms are constructed with a random mix cipher alphabet and normal plaintext alphabet. As a matter of fact, many constructors who sell to puzzle magazines and newspaper syndicates don't know there are other (and more interesting) ways to construct. Some of these varieties in construction make solving more fun. The cipher-keyed cryptogram is one.

The crypts in this chapter were constructed with a cipher alphabet keyword. As you'll see, the keyword serves as extra challenge and as solving aid simultaneously.

The challenge: Pit your wits against the constructor's. See if you can recover the keyword he used, as well as solve the cryptogram.

The solving aid: The solver who takes the trouble of writing out the alphabets may find he can quickly learn the identity of some cipher letters.

Here's how it works.

Suppose you are solving a crypt containing the cipher pattern word PNDDVF, which you guess to be CANNOT:

```
P N D D V F
C A N N O T
```

You set up your two alphabets, as described in Chapter 2, this way:

```
Cipher: N   P                       D V         F
Plain:  A B C D E F G H I J K L M N O P Q R S T U V W X Y Z
```

You know that the top (cipher) alphabet must contain all 26 letters of the alphabet, and that the crypts in this chapter are based on cipher-keyed alphabets. That means the cipher alphabet contains a keyword, followed by the normal alphabet in order, except that those letters used in the keyword are not repeated.

Examining your alphabets, you note the positions of the top letters. N blank P—that could be part of the keyword, or part of the normal alphabet. Looking further, you see DV. Since these letters are not consecutive, you know that your keyword is here and that DV is part of it. (Perhaps you can think of a word right off the bat with DV in it.) The F appears to be part of the normal alphabet, and N and P a continuation.

So you know immediately that you can safely insert a cipher O between the N and P. If there are any other cipher O's in the cipher, you can write B underneath and proceed with solving.

By working back and forth between solving the cryptogram and filling in the cipher alphabet, you can recover the entire constructor's alphabet and keyword.

Should you run into a snag because all of the 26 letters of the cipher alphabet do not appear in the cryptogram, use logic, reason, guesswork and common sense. (We never promised you a rose garden.)

## PROBLEMS FOR SOLVING

### 1. Philosophical View

*I F W O J S  O W  N M J  S O X W ' A

I J W:  "E M X J U J B  M F A  N X  V F R J

N M J  F K N J B–I O W W J B

B J V F B R A,  N M F W R  L X X I W J A A

O N  E X W ' N  G J  V J!"

*Cipher:*
*Plain:* A B C D E F G H I J K L M N O P Q R S T U V W X Y Z

(Clues: Pattern match for IOWWJB is in the Appendix.)

**2. Infernal Revenue**

Y U L O J C M A S R S R D Q B Y M O X

L A S B L I S O U A M C M D A B L I S-

W M C S E L J, C L O J M U D X

G Y N N O M B W L F S L W M C S B M

B L I S Y B B M.

*Cipher:*
*Plain:* A B C D E F G H I J K L M N O P Q R S T U V W X Y Z

(Clues: Note one-letter word. See pattern match for GYNN in the Appendix.)

**3. Strange Way to Write**

Q F A R G U Y D A U: Y F W S K A P A F O

Q M A F O G F D W G F I R G S I D

P C K G Q O C G Q P M Q U C Y M

"H I K M I R I K I, W I H I K V I U P

E I F, I R I K B I I H P C I

H K I U I H P M P I F."

*Cipher:*
*Plain:* A B C D E F G H I J K L M N O P Q R S T U V W X Y Z

(Clues: Notice the frequency of cipher I. What might it represent? See pattern match for BIIH in the Appendix.)

**4. Silence Is Golden**

L E R J R  X J R  L Q G  A N F P K  G U

N F L R B B N D R F L  H R G H B R,

L E G K R  Q N L E  R F G M D E  Q N L

L G  L X B A  Q R B B  X F P  L E G K R

Q N L E  R F G M D E  N F K N D E L  L G

Y R  K N B R F L.

*Cipher:*
*Plain:* A B C D E F G H I J K L M N O P Q R S T U V W X Y Z

(Clue: Keyword is PRUDENT.)

**5. Crepe Hanger**

M E  P T L X K X A L  K M H  A R R  M

S X V W L  F W R C R  L W R C R  X A

E P E R,  N B L  F W H  K B A L  L W R

T R A A X K X A L  M S F M H A  C B E  L P

N S P F  X L  P B L?  *K X O W R S  Q R

*A M X E L–T X R C C R

*Cipher:*
*Plain:* A B C D E F G H I J K L M N O P Q R S T U V W X Y Z

(Clues: What is the one-letter word M? Use that to guess at the first word in the crypt. From there go to word EPER. If you need more help, try looking up a pattern word.)

**6. Mind Your P's and Q's**

R Y R   K C F   X T O B   O P C F E   E X T

Q X F B Q X   C B W O I Y D E   H X C

E C C M   O I   T J E B O   Z C P   O D

Z O I Y E C B?   I C H   X T ' D   P F D K

S Y I R Y I W   X Y D   M T K D   O I R

A T H D.

*Cipher:*
*Plain:* A B C D E F G H I J K L M N O P Q R S T U V W X Y Z

(Clues: Note question mark. Can you guess at the first word? Check pattern words in the Appendix. Don't forget to fill in the alphabet as you go along—it's a great solving aid, and anyway you want to recover the keyword.)

**7. Naughty Words**

N F   C H   F X U S   X E   T D S S R H U   H T

E A S S Q W   U H D S   A D S Q X H G E

F W N C   J W S C   N   U N C   W X F E   W X E

F W G U P   J X F W   N   W N U U S D.

*U N D E W N O O   *O G U E R S C.

*Cipher:*
*Plain:* A B C D E F G H I J K L M N O P Q R S T U V W X Y Z

(Clues: Note one-letter word. Then go to first word. You may find a pattern word in the back of the book, if you need one.)

**8. Upper Class**

A P V M  P G  E W G  F O Z E,  "S F

G O S F  V Z Y  E W V S Y D W W V?"

V W P A W D:  "M W F,  S X  O W  U Z H A V

G P A R  O W  K Z H A V I ' G  F E W P R

G Z  W S G O W D  Z X  H F."

*Cipher:*
*Plain:* A B C D E F G H I J K L M N O P Q R S T U V W X Y Z

(Clues: Note apostrophe. What might GZ be? Place those letters in the blank cipher alphabet. Does that provide any further clues?)

# 4
# PLAINTEXT-KEYED CRYPTOGRAMS

"The thing can be done," said the Butcher, "I think,
"The thing must be done, I am sure.
"The thing shall be done! Bring me paper and ink,
"The best there is time to procure."

*The Hunting of the Snark*

Plaintext-keyed cryptograms are constructed exactly opposite of the ciphertext-keyed ones.

The constructor sets up a normal alphabet to represent cipher letters, and uses a keyed alphabet for the equivalent plaintext letters. Again, the object for the solver is to not only solve the cipher, but to also recover the keyword used in the constructor's plaintext alphabet.

Proceed by filling in letters in the blank plain alphabet as you find them. If you need any help, clues are given at the end of the chapter.

## PROBLEMS FOR SOLVING

### 1. Lazy Louts

L T  L E  P O C F L P O M  D A Y O

O T T A P E  E A  U A  T P A Y  E A M Q J

E A  E A Y A P P A H,  D A Y O  B O A B N O

H A F N M  Q N H Q J D  P O Y Q L Z  L Z

J O D E O P M Q J.

*Cipher:* A B C D E F G H I J K L M N O P Q R S T U V W X Y Z
*Plain:*

### 2. Smart Move

R T S Y G Q *Y R N Y T R F X T N S X Q

E Y O X S Y N Q T. S X Q J P T R T O Q N

S B O Q S E Y N B W *P T R X T S S T R

U Q W B E Q S X Q J X T N S B C T J

S T I Q F B R Y S.

*Cipher:* A B C D E F G H I J K L M N O P Q R S T U V W X Y Z
*Plain:*

### 3. Retaliation

W N Y N F P N G H J R G F M U O

Z G S M Q E H X G L N, Z I G L I X I N

T U W N J T J F ' H F J X E W N

W E F H X U, X I N T U W N U E P I X

S J Z X U Z N N M G X U E X.

*O W J F L G H *K J L U F.

*Cipher:* A B C D E F G H I J K L M N O P Q R S T U V W X Y Z
*Plain:*

### 4. Doubtful Praise

G E T E D E L L K W F

J E S U R O S K T D F T G F X Q F

L F Z E W F D D N K X F S K D O S K.

F JESUROSKTD DNFD OX

JNFWMKG LEW OX TED

ZFRYFIRK. *SFWQ *DAFOT.

*Cipher:* ABCDEFGHIJKLMNOPQRSTUVWXYZ
*Plain:*

**5. Be Flexible!**

INPG NV: QCE FNSW, UYWNM,

VECM SWNQ GNTSW, SWNHWF

CMWP GC FWNG WOXYG

MWCMSW, YOPXW YCSVF GYWB

QOEBSK OP MSNUW.

*Cipher:* ABCDEFGHIJKLMNOPQRSTUVWXYZ
*Plain:*

**6. Political Independent**

Q *YLUELYK VQB MJJR

SJTORJS QB Q MOIS EVZ

BOCB EOCV VOB YLU ZR ZRJ

BOSJ ZT CVJ TJRPJ QRS

VOB ELYK ZR CVJ ZCVJI.

*Cipher:* ABCDEFGHIJKLMNOPQRSTUVWXYZ
*Plain:*

**7. Prolific Writer**

*C L H C  *M Y Z W H C P  *E Z L U W C L

R T L G C U  T W  Z M  I Z W P  Z M

M C N C W  A T T G M  Z Y  T W C  Y X I C

Z W U  R L T Y C  T W C  S V W U L C U

Z W U  D T L Y P  W T N C H M  U V L X W E

S X M  H X D C Y X I C.

*Cipher:* A B C D E F G H I J K L M N O P Q R S T U V W X Y Z
*Plain:*

**8. Making It Unanimous?**

M T I  M Y D X  Y R  *Y X Y C K P P I,

*X. *Q.  D N A  A Y  X N W I J

O I L N B A I  I N L T  M K W I  N

X N W I  D N A  A B S S I A M I J  N M  N

L Y B X L K P  W I I M K X S,  M T I H I

D N A  N  L T Y H B A  Y R  "Y T,  X Y" A.

*Cipher:* A B C D E F G H I J K L M N O P Q R S T U V W X Y Z
*Plain:*

(Clues: The crutch of pattern words was not provided for these crypts so that those solvers wanting to learn techniques could rely on their own ingenuity to crack the codes. However, if you were stumped on any, here is some help.)

**1.** Did you fail to recognize that pattern word BOABNO? It has appeared before and often appears in cryptograms. Look for it in the back of the book.

**2.** Look for pattern word YRNYTRF in back of book.

**3.** Alphabet keyword begins with the plaintext letter P.

**4.** Here's that common word DNFD again.

**5.** Once more, MWCMSW (same pattern as Problem 1's BOABNO). What is it?

**6.** Term given to a bolter from the Republican party in 1884 is contained in this cipher.

**7.** You'll find the pattern word for MCNCW in the back.

**8.** When a three-letter word begins a sentence, that word is usually what?

# 5
# MISCELLANEOUS TYPES

Norman looked gloomy. "Give me time," he said, "I must think it over."

*A Tangled Tale*

All cryptograms, including those in the preceding chapters, can be solved without writing out the coding alphabets, without knowing how the cryptogram was constructed and without recovering the keyword, if any.

But writing out the alphabets always reveals something about the cryptogram helpful to the solver. At the very least, it's a good way to keep track of what letters have been found. It's also fun to find out what method the constructor used in his efforts to baffle you—or to give you, tongue in cheek, a helping hand.

A surprise awaits those who will take the trouble to begin filling in the blank alphabets in the following four cryptograms. You won't even have to finish the alphabets before you quickly see something that should cut your solving time in half.

## PROBLEMS FOR SOLVING

### 1. Wish You Were Here

Z IVZO UIRVMW RH

HLNVLMV DSL GZPVH Z

DRMGVI EZXZGRLM LM Z

HFM-WIVMXSVW YVZXS ZMW

WLVHM'G HVMW Z XZIW.

*U Z I N V I H *Z O N Z M Z X

*Cipher:*
*Plain:* A B C D E F G H I J K L M N O P Q R S T U V W X Y Z

**2. But Not Homogenized**

K V H H R N R H G R X I V N Z I P: G S V

N R O P L U S F N Z M P R M W M V H H

R H H L N V G R N V H H P R N N V W,

H L N V G R N V H X L M W V M H V W,

Y F G N L H G L U G V M

V E Z K L I Z G V W.

*Cipher:*
*Plain:* A B C D E F G H I J K L M N O P Q R S T U V W X Y Z

**3. Unjustified Accusation?**

N *A R J *L B E X C H O Y V F U R E

O E B H T U G B H G N I B Y H Z R B S

O Y N A X C N T R F P N Y Y R Q "*G U R

*A B G U V A T *O B B X" N A Q J N F

N P P H F R Q B S C Y N T V N E V F Z.

*Cipher:*
*Plain:* A B C D E F G H I J K L M N O P Q R S T U V W X Y Z

**4. Geography Note**

G U R *Z N Y Q V I R V F Y N A Q F

P B A F V F G B S G U B H F N A Q F B S

Y H F U P B E N Y N G B Y Y F V A

G U R *V A Q V N A *B P R N A. Z N A L

N E R H A V A U N O V G R Q.

*Cipher:*
*Plain:* A B C D E F G H I J K L M N O P Q R S T U V W X Y Z

(Clue: Did you notice the code word GUR in Problem 3, and here again? How come?)

Besides random mix, alphabet shift, ciphertext-keyed, plaintext-keyed and reciprocal alphabets, are there other ways to construct a cryptogram? Yes. The encoder may use *two* keyed alphabets, with the same keyword for each. Or he may use two keyed alphabets with a different keyword for each.

The purpose of keywords is to shield the cipher from prying eyes while providing the intended recipient of the message with a key for quick and easy deciphering. If a scrambled alphabet were used, the recipient of the message would have to solve it from scratch or keep a written copy of the scrambled alphabet. With a keyword, he simply memorizes the key, and uses it each time he receives a message.

How about a cryptogram using real letters—no substitutions? Is there a way to mask a message when the actual letters are to be used? Certainly. Here is a very simple cipher of that sort. The letters of the message are all here, but not in normal order. Can you decode it?

**5. The Way to Get Nowhere**

S R E N R O C Y N A M O O T G N I

T T U C Y L B A B O R P S I S E

L C R I C   N I   D N U   O R A

G N I O G F L E S M   I H   S D N   I F O H

W Y D O   B Y N A.

(Clue: Turnabout is fair play.)

**6. Long Nap**

N K W O   H W R Y   P I A V   W N N I

L K W E   S A B A   E L O T   L S E E

F P R O   W T N E   Y T E Y   R A N S

N O O E   H F S I   E N G I   B H R O

H S D A   S A E T   E R P O   A L E Y   R.

(Clue: Study the first group of letters.)

**7. Courage**

W A H T W C   E O M O M N   L C Y A L B

L R A E V R   Y S I N O T   T H E A L C

K F O F E R   A B U I T T   S O C N Q E

U S T Y S D   N Y E H A R   R I S.

(Clue: Do you need one?)

**8. Value System**

F I U O Y   A C P S N   N E P A D   R E C E F

L T S U Y   L E S S E   F A R E T   O N I N O

```
ANREP EFLTC UYLES SEAMS

NNYRE UOVAH LERAE ENOHD

TWILO EV.
```

(Clue: Again, study the first group of letters.)

Cryptograms in which one letter of the alphabet consistently represents another letter are "simple substitution" cryptograms. Those in which the actual letters are concealed by moving them about are called "transposition" cryptograms (or ciphers).

In the next two chapters we'll go back to simple subs again, and then proceed to more sophisticated and difficult versions of both substitution and transposition ciphers.

# 6
# HARDER CRYPTOGRAMS

The Red Queen shook her head. "You may call it nonsense if you like," she said, "but I've heard nonsense, compared with which that would be as sensible as a dictionary!"

*Through the Looking-Glass*

What makes a cryptogram difficult to solve?

Generally, it's the absence of those factors that make it easy to solve: one-letter words, common words such as "the," easy-to-identify pattern words such as "that" and "people" and deliberate alteration of normal frequency counts. Omitting such giveaways is a fair tactic.

Unfair tactics, sometimes used by unknowledgeable constructors who, one suspects, could not solve their own miserable concoctions under penalty of death, include too-short cryptograms, not enough different letters used, too many singletons (letters used but once) and weird texts such as "Amblyopic, purblind gourmand, bursting stomach edgy, thumped bulgy chyme batch alongside pylorus sphincter."

The eight cryptograms in this chapter are fairly constructed. All are of reasonable length and contain a sufficient number of different letters. None contains more than four singletons. Some contain pattern words. Some contain the word "the" or other common short words to be used as opening wedges. One contains a one-letter word. Yet, for one reason or another, you may find these difficult. Alphabets are not provided, but if you get stuck, do try writing them out. Or see if you can find a pattern word or non-pattern word in the Appendix, that fits. Reread the basic rules for solving on page 8 and refer to "A Bag of Tricks" in the Appendix for more help.

## PROBLEMS FOR SOLVING

### 1. Bird Lore

Q E L P B  T E L  P E L R I A  H K L T

P X V  Q E B  L P Q O F Z E  A L B P

K L Q  Y R O V  F Q P  E B X A  F K  Q E B

P X K A  Q L  E F A B.  Y R Q  Q E B

J V Q E  F P  E X O A  Q L  A F P M B I.

(Clues: The most common digraph—sequence of two letters—in English is TH. Do you see a frequently occurring digraph here? If you need more help, this crypt contains many two- and three-letter words. Check the short non-pattern word lists in the Appendix.)

### 2. Keep Umbrella Unfurled

P Z Q H L A  R X Z  O Q L W S

D Q A A Q M A  K V I P Q  X W  Q I Z A N

S X Q M  A X  *J X B W A

*D I L I L Q I V Q  L W  *U I B I L,

*N I D I L L,  D N Q Z Q  N Q I C F

Z I L W M  R I V V  W Q I Z V F  Q C Q Z F

H I F.

(Clues: Note pattern words—you may find one of them in the back. Compare XW, LW and AX. This crypt contains unusual vowel clusters.)

**3. Crackerjack**

D X Y U V  H L O C T  L N B F A R

M O B Q C,  A B D U T  X B Q C  T X B S,

Q B P U T  M L Q C  H X U A  R L N C,

S Y Q C T  O B Q C,  E F Y Q C O J

S L Q C T  T D B Q C  Y A  C A L S T L Q C.

(Clues: Did you note the title? Note repetition of digraph QC. When a cipher letter appears only at the end of a word, and only once, that letter is usually Y. Normal frequencies are distorted here—E appears only a few times.)

**4. This One's Tricky**

R  V O A C O Q I X O A Z J V  M Y V

G U M A J–H U O C O Q I  D M Y M Q J Y

M Q D J  A C R U C J V  C M  G X N Y O A Z

R  W M Y M Q J Y,  N X C  K X O C . . .

C Z J  J L G J Q A J  H R A

O Q T M Y M Q J Y!

(Clues: Start with that one-letter word, go to HRA. If normal frequencies hold, which cipher letter is E? As the title warns, there's a trick or two played here.)

**5. Page Benjamin Franklin**

S E U  H R D Y  A N J  A V K  Q N O D.

Y N U C  A R D Y  G O Z N U J  E Z V F U C

L V R O E J D  Y N Z D,  H N Z D  A Z V Q D

V F O,  Z E J D C  H V Z  M V F Z G,

A F Z U D C  C V Y U  M V S D G.

(Clues: Letter frequencies are somewhat distorted in this crypt, but E retains its number-one position. The title may help. Cipher K, by the way, does not represent Y here. If desperate, you'll find GOZNUJ in the non-pattern word list.)

### 6. How's That Again?

P T U K A K D K N A  N U  "Q B N A L T":

R A  T G B R A Q K J Y T

R J Q N O B D K N A  Z N P E Y T

Q T A Q K D K F T  D N

P K U U T O T A D K R Y  Z N Y T S E Y R O

D T A Q K N A Q.

(Clues: Compare NU and DN. A pattern word is included in the Appendix.)

### 7. Strike Out on Your Own

M L G R X V  S L D  L U G V M  G S V

B L F M T  N Z M  D S L  O V U G  S L N V

G L  H V G  G S V  D L I O W  L M  U R I V

S Z W  G L  X L N V  Y Z X P  G L  T V G

N L I V  N Z G X S V H?

(Clues: Note SLD. and DSL. Check the three-letter non-pattern words to identify these.)

**8. Gone With the Wind**

K Z D F L V Y E A T  D Z B P V J S K X

O X S K D  F S K D L V Y Q G W,

K Z D B L I Y Q G F  L S G T Q F.  O Z Y F

G X Z B P V L  G W S D B L V

O E A T V P S Y D L,  D Z B P V W G Y Q

J X Z B P V  Q D F L.

(Clues: This cryptogram contains unusual consonant clusters—groups of three, four and even five consonants unbroken by a vowel. You'll find one of the non-pattern words in the Appendix if you absolutely have to have it.)

# 7
# UNDIVIDED CRYPTOGRAMS

"It's perfectly intelligible," the Captain said in an offended tone, "to anyone who understands such things."

*A Tangled Tale*

The cryptograms preceding this chapter could have been made much more difficult to solve by the simple expedient of concealing the lengths of words. This can be done by grouping the letters in groups (five is customary) and omitting punctuation.

The eight cryptograms in this chapter are so presented. The solver thus loses the usefulness of short words, pattern words and similar aids to solving.

To solve an "undivided" cipher, take a frequency count (the number of times each letter appears). Note the repeated digraphs and reversed digraphs (see the Appendix). It helps to circle low-frequency letters (those appearing one to three times). Letters adjacent to low-frequency letters, especially if these adjacent letters are of high frequency, are usually vowels. Try to guess the vowels first, acting on the assumption that the letter appearing most often is a vowel and probably E. For those who need them, pattern words are provided. It's up to you to figure out their placement by searching the cipher for that pattern.

## PROBLEMS FOR SOLVING

### 1. Easy Does It

GSVIF OVRMX ZIERM TSLOW

HTLLW ZHGLX IRGRX RHNMV

EVIXF GDRGS ZPMRU VDSZG

BLFXZ MXFGD RGSZH KLLMZ

C R L N U  I L N X S  Z I O V H  Y F C G L

M.

(Clues: The letter appearing most often is a vowel, but not E. The pattern word CRITICISM appears in the plaintext.)

**2. A Matter of Geology**

U M E B M  L S I X I  S D K A S  E Q S I D

M U X D B  S J X B D  S I Q S M  F E A C O

I S D B S  S L B D M  W O G S W  O R I M X

Q S O D O  C C O D S  X D W S E  D W S I M

E D W M E  D W S B M  F D W A M  C S.

(Clues: When a three-letter sequence appears more than once in an undivided, and when the last of these three letters is of high frequency, that three-letter sequence could be the word THE. Pattern word PERCENT appears in the plaintext.)

**3. If Youth But Knew**

N J M N X  H J O X S  J I I P A  S J J V N

X D W I E  H E B S X  N E W H I  S D H B U

E B F J G  X U J E I  M P I J E  S I P A S

B E I N J  S N X D L  N S N P U  I J T K E

S S M J V  S B K W X  U U E W B  M P T I X

V T P S S  T J.

(Clues: Pattern word THOUGHT appears in the plaintext. Examine the cipher for the TH-HT pattern.)

**4. Creative Souls**

F N E Q N   L O O K L   F L D K O   E D U D K

U S U K M   H X O A T   E H N L U   D D E S H

R E N O A   T E N L V   L J R J E   D S L D R

U E D H D   K P H O T   U E D R T   L U N E A

D A E N X   K O K N A   H C D L K   C L N.

(Clues: Singletons are cipher letters PQVM, representing plaintext letters FGJU. If you need help, lay out your two alphabets. More help? A seven-letter pattern word is provided in the Appendix.)

**5. Sir Galahad to the Rescue**

I Y A I S   F W Z B U   B J L A X   W V J A X

O B L Y B   V N S J N   D J S N Y   I S J Z P

U U B V Q   W V Y B T   I Y V A A   I S Q A M

B M Q P L   Y F A J A   I V B I S   J N F W R

A V B M B   Q W T A V   J Y S N Y   F W R A V

A T X P U   U A I.

(Clues: Most frequent letter is E. You'll find a five-letter pattern word for this crypt under 12344 in the Appendix.)

**6. Orderly Words**

P H K W R   H W M I A   F D A Y H   J A D U J

P U G X G   H R X Q I   U J D Q L   F D T X A

```
U Y D Q H   W M X W D   W X D T I   A X S U H

K I D T I   A X J A U   H K I D W   I X J U H

K I D J M   P D Y X A   U H K I.
```

(Clues: You'll find the plaintext sequence IOUS appearing four times. A four-letter pattern word can be found under 1231 in the Appendix.)

**7. Oratory**

```
R F K R W   U C Q V K   S Y R F A   U E K H C

Q V Y D A   H K I O K   W A Y A R   F I R R F

K W K Y A   R U U E C   D F V K J   T R F R U

R F K Y W   A H K K D   F K A I J   X J U R K

J U C T F   X K H R F.
```

(Clues: Remember what digraph is often of high frequency? Here it is again. After guessing at that digraph and then at the first word of the crypt, you may be able to solve this without further help. If help is needed, refer to the Appendix for pattern word 12343.)

**8. The Gold Bug Cipher**

In 1843 Edgar Allan Poe won a $100 prize for his story "The Gold Bug," the plot of which hinges on a mysterious cipher. The story has intrigued readers ever since.

If you read the story, you were probably baffled by the cipher. No wonder. Numbers and symbols all run together—very confusing.

With minor revisions (changing certain symbols) here is the cipher as Poe presented it:

```
53##+305))6*;4826)4#.)4#);806*;48+8/60))
85;1#(;:#*8+83(88)5*+;46(;88*96*?;8)*#(;
```

485);5*+2:*#(;4956*2(5*-4)8/8*;4069285);
)6+8)4##;1(#9;48081;8:8#1;48+85;4)485+52
8806*81(#9;48;(88;4(#?34;48)4#;161;:188;
#?;

Could you solve such a formidable cipher? Of course! If you take this gibberish and consider it calmly, you may decide it's an ordinary "simple substitution" cryptogram, of the very kind we've been doing in this chapter—undivided.

Counting the number of different symbols, you would find there are 20—just about right if each symbol and number represents a different letter of the alphabet. (Letters like Q, X and Z appear infrequently, along with others, so a random sample of English writing will usually contain only 17 to 21 different letters.)

Feeling rather sure of yourself now, you would rewrite the cipher in groups of five. You would also set up a pair of substitution alphabets and count the frequencies of each symbol.

53##+ 305)) 6*;48 26)4#

.)4#) ;806* ;48+8 /60))

85;1# (;:#* 8+83( 88)5*

+;46( ;88*9 6*?;8 )*#(;

485); 5*+2: *#(;4 956*2

(5*-4 )8/8* ;4069 285);

)6+8) 4##;1 (#9;4 8081;

8:8#1 ;48+8 5;4)4 85+52

8806* 81(#9 ;48;( 88;4(

#?34; 48)4# ;161; :188;

#?;

*Cipher*: 0 1 2 3 4 5 6 8 9 * : . ; ? # + / ( ) -
*Plain*:

Taking a frequency count, you would write the following frequencies over the cipher alphabet: 0 – 6, 1 – 8, 2 – 5, 3 – 4, 4 – 19, 5 – 12, 6 – 11, 8 – 33, 9 – 5, * – 13, : – 4, . – 1, ; – 26, ? – 3, # – 16, + – 8, / – 2, ( – 10, ) – 16 and – – 1.

The letter appearing most frequently in a simple substitution crypt is usually E. Looking over your frequencies, you decide which number or symbol you will try, first, for E.

Next, you may recall that the most commonly recurring digraph is TH and examine the crypt for recurring pairs of symbols.

You then realize that your guesses so far are quite likely correct, because the word THE emerges. And when you've placed all the T, H, E's under their cipher equivalents, you find, joyfully, that you already have more than one third of this "formidable" cipher solved.

Should you follow in the footsteps of Poe's Mr. Legrand, you will next discover the identity of R and, simultaneously, G, U and O.

Or you may go off on a tack of your own, knowing the yet-unidentified high-frequency symbols probably represent A, O and I. Since A and I rarely double (AARDVARK and RADII and such being exceptions), if you have a high-frequency symbol that appears doubled, it may be O.

Try solving the Gold Bug Cipher. You're off to a good start. (More Clues: Several numbers appear in the cipher. The cipher translates to rather enigmatic directions to a buried treasure of gold and jewels.)

# 8
# KEY PHRASE CIPHERS

"That is not said right," said the Caterpillar. "Not quite right," said Alice timidly, "some of the words have got altered."

*Alice's Adventures in Wonderland*

It was entirely in character for Edgar Allan Poe to write a story based on a cipher. He was deeply interested in codes and ciphers and was quite an expert.

In 1841 Poe had some fun playing around with a type of cryptogram known as the Key Phrase Cipher. That year he wrote a book review for *Graham's Lady's and Gentleman's Magazine* in Philadelphia. The book contained a description of a coded note sent to a duchess, the key to the cipher being, not a cipher alphabet but a 26-letter phrase.

Poe explained the workings of this kind of cipher to his readers, then invited them to submit such ciphers to him. He "pledged" himself "for the solution of the riddle" and did, in fact, decipher most of the crypts sent to him.

The Key Phrase departs from the ordinary cryptogram in three ways:

**1.** A letter may represent itself.
**2.** A cipher letter may represent more than one plaintext letter.
**3.** The encoder uses a 26-letter sentence or phrase as his ciphering key rather than a disarranged cipher alphabet.

Here's an example of Key Phrase alphabets, as offered by Poe in one of his writings. He is showing off a bit by using a Latin sentence:

*Cipher:* F O R T I T E R I N R E S U A V I T E R I N M O D O
*Plain:* A B C D E F G H I J K L M N O P Q R S T U V W X Y Z

The Latin reads *fortiter in re, suaviter in modo*—"strongly in deed, gently in manner."

To encode the word GAMES from Poe's cipher key, substitute

for plain G a cipher E, for plain A cipher F and so on, resulting in the word EFSIE.

Here is another example, this time in English:

*Cipher:* A N E X A M P L E O F K E Y P H R A S E C I P H E R
*Plain:* A B C D E F G H I J K L M N O P Q R S T U V W X Y Z

See how this makes deciphering more difficult? In the above, cipher A stands for plain A, and cipher S for plain S. Thus a cipher letter can stand for any of 26 letters instead of 25.

Note how many times cipher E appears in the top sentence. It represents five different plaintext letters. This throws the frequency count off and confuses the poor solver. The cipher word for CITY, for instance (four different plaintext letters), becomes EEEE (is that a mouse's squeak or a shoe size?).

Finally, note that many letters of the alphabet are missing from the cipher key. If they were all present, we would have a simple one-to-one substitution of letters.

To solve the Key Phrases in this chapter, work back and forth between key sentence (cipher "alphabet") and cryptogram. Guess at probable words in the crypt and try them out in both crypt and cipher key, and vice versa.

Important: Keep firmly in mind that one cipher letter may stand for several plaintext letters, but each plaintext letter has but one cipher substitute. If that's not clear, study the alphabets above. It's easy to get confused here.

Now, if you like, pretend you are the great Edgar Allan Poe and that your readers have sent you the following muddles to untangle. Can you do it?

## PROBLEMS FOR SOLVING

### 1. The Doorway to Success

T E   F E E   S R T L   R E S L E T R F S

A L   I L T L A R L   K E A   T E   F E E

```
R A T T L L T   R S S L T R L E L E K.


G L S L S I L G   R E   S L K   I L   E T L


E L R E   K L K   E T L E   E L L F R   E T L


E E T K.
```

*Cipher:* I L S G
*Plain:* A B C D E F G H I J K L M N O P Q R S T U V W X Y Z

(Clues: The word REMEMBER appears in the plaintext. Note that words in Key Phrase ciphers which appear to be pattern words may not be. (Remember CITY = EEEE in the example?) However, these Key Phrases have been coded so that the pattern words offered as clues can be readily identified. As you solve, you will find you are placing several plaintext letters under one cipher letter. FEE, in fact (cipher word in above crypt) will show up like this:

```
F E E
-----
N T T
  F F
  L L
  O O
```

It's up to you to pick the right letter from each vertical group to spell out the correct plaintext word. Here, the right word is NOT. We've left plenty of space beneath the cipher rows for your multiple entries. Can you solve the cipher and also recover the key sentence? The key (cipher) sentence here is a familiar proverb. The letters for REMEMBER have been placed for you in the cipher alphabet.

Distribute the plaintext letters REMB throughout the cipher.

For further help, refer to the FEE table above. Alphabet: Place a cipher E above letters TLFO in the plaintext alphabet, and place a cipher F above the letter N. Cipher: Distribute the plaintext letters NTLFO. Under every E in the cipher write all four letters TFLO, and under every F write an N. When you have this done, examine the cipher. See any possible words? How about ETL—if you guess at that, also try your guess out on ETLE. Examine the incomplete cipher alphabet. Does a familiar quotation come to mind? If so, test it. Work back and forth between the cipher and the cipher "alphabet" or key sentence.)

**2. Evelyn Wood for Drivers?**

V E T  E E T T A  S E R S E V S R T  S A

D O T T E  A T S E T E R  T D  V E S V

T V  T E S W U T D  T S E  V S

A T R E A T  S E V  V E T

E U S R T A U T S A  D T R E D  T E  V T S T.

*Cipher:*
*Plain:* A B C D E F G H I J K L M N O P Q R S T U V W X Y Z

(Clues: The word SPEED is in the plaintext. Consider the clue word, SPEED, along with the title. Does that suggest a word that might follow SPEED? Look at the first word in the cipher. When a three-letter word starts a cipher, that word is often what?)

**3. Limits of Knowledge**

L T O L A O O O  O N  O N E  T S E  T O

F N O E N  O I L  H E S O L  O I

A E T O O L E  O N E A E  T A E  L I A E

O N O L S N  O I L  R I L ' O  O L I F

O N T L  O I L  R I.

*Cipher:*
*Plain:* A B C D E F G H I J K L M N O P Q R S T U V W X Y Z

(Clues: Look for pattern word to match ONEAE in the Appendix, if you need it. First, though, use this tip: Cipher O stands for six plaintext letters, which accounts for the high frequency of O in the cipher. These plaintext letters are IKLTXY.)

**4. Handsome Salary**

A B E  B A A V  A E V  V P E H  E E T E

A B E  V P E H  E B E L  E A N T

B T E P A E H A  P R R E A E A L  E P H

A A  E P T L  A B E  H P E P T E  E A N

O P L L A A  E E N E  A L  L A E.

*Cipher:*
*Plain:* A B C D E F G H I J K L M N O P Q R S T U V W X Y Z

(Clues: You'll find a pattern word to match BTEPAEHA in the Appendix. Look at the triple appearance of ABE—and it's also the first word. What word might you suspect it to be?)

**5. Vision**

E T N  H A A  A A F T O H,  H T F  E T N

H H E  "O A E?"  A N A  F  F T A H E

A A F T O H  A A H A  T A N A T  O A T A,

H T F  F  H H E  "O A E  T T A?"

*A A T T H T F  *H A H O

*Cipher:*
*Plain:* A B C D E F G H I J K L M N O P Q R S T U V W X Y Z

(Clues: Okay, now—there's a three-letter word starting this cipher and it appears twice. But remember that what is true for a majority may not be true for a minority. Also, that one-letter word may be A or it may not. Ciphers are insidious things which can trip you up just when you think you've mastered a technique. Concentrate on the three-letter word followed by a question mark. Isn't it likely to be HOW or WHY? A pattern word to match HAA can be found in the Appendix. In solving, use a null X in the cipher alphabet for plaintext Z.)

**6. Just the Facts, Please**

H I  H T  H R U R  U U R H

E T U R C R T T A R T T  T H R T I

I U T I H  I H T A  U U R H

H A I R A I H R A T C  C H H A T  I H T I

I H R U R  H T  T R  H T E H

U T C T R H R R T  H A  I H R  S R U C T.

H H  *T T H T R C  *A R H A T R A

*Cipher:*
*Plain:* A B C D E F G H I J K L M N O P Q R S T U V W X Y Z

(Clue: A word to match ETURCRTTARTT can be found in the Appendix.)

**7. Worth More**

H D W *H K E B A D T K M T A D T W N W R

R S N W T K N T S E H T K T T T R

B K E D K T T S L I E W T T S E R T

I W T H T A W D A T T E D S B, I A H

D W A D T T T W K R T K R S E D

A T R D T I H K S E T W E W N W E.

*Cipher:*
*Plain:* A B C D E F G H I J K L M N O P Q R S T U V W X Y Z

(Clues: Note the one-letter word. Note the three-letter word that begins the cipher. If a pattern word is needed, look up TKMT in the Appendix.)

**8. Self-Torture**

Here, to test your mettle, is an undivided key phrase.

A O B N N B H A N T R H A O N A T N R R

O G R H N A N R E H R A N R E A R N R A

N R T T R E E N H N R E N R O A E A R A

O E H R N H R O H B O A N B H T R T C E

B H N N B T R E O N N B G A T R T

*Cipher:*
*Plain:* A B C D E F G H I J K L M N O P Q R S T U V W X Y Z

(Clue: The name of an animal can be found in the plaintext. It's a small, nocturnal animal covered with stout spines.)

# 9
# NULL CIPHERS

"If any of them can explain it," said Alice . . . "I'll give him sixpence. I don't believe there's an atom of meaning in it."

*Alice's Adventures in Wonderland*

A Null Cipher can be easy or difficult. The Null is a cipher in which some of the letters (usually the majority) are purposeless, put in to confuse and conceal. We call these useless letters nulls. The remaining letters are original plaintext letters, not substitutions.

During World War I, the Germans used null ciphers. In his monumental work *The Codebreakers* David Kahn offers the following example of a German cipher:

```
Apparently, neutral's protest is thoroughly
discounted and ignored. Isman hard hit.
Blockade issue affects pretext for embargo on
byproducts, ejecting suets and vegetable
oils.
```

To decode the message, read only the second letter of each word. All other letters are nulls. NY=New York.

Null cover messages need not make sense. When real words are used, as above, in an effort to make the message seem legitimate, the resultant wording often sounds stilted and odd.

Nulls may consist of series of letters spelling out nothing (except the coded message). They may be lists of related or unrelated words. Any number of schemes may be used. The encoder might use the first letter of the first word, the second letter of the second word, the third letter of the third word and then repeat the series. Or the sequence could depend on letters rather than words: skip the first two letters, read the third, and so on.

## PROBLEMS FOR SOLVING

### 1. Good for Any Business

(The following wire amused the manager of a small factory where scrap losses had been excessive.)

We are soon to enlarge night operations. Temporary workers all now transferred. Notify our trainees.

### 2. Tout de Suite

(Note mailed to a conspirator.)

CUCKOO GAMBLE PEANUT SPOKEN DECODE

### 3. Grocery List

(Found in the pocket of a suspected terrorist.)

pudding mix, any kind
fryer, 4–5 lbs.
tuna fish
spaghetti
ham
chili powder
dates
cherry pie
cabbage
margarine
raisins
haddock
Baggies
bread (rye or whole wheat)
ketchup
flour
Sanka coffee (drip)
juice, orange or grapefruit
sugar, 5 lbs.
kohlrabi if the store has it
lettuce

### 4. Reverse English?

(Johnny's dad, who is teaching him cryptology, rearranged the words in Johnny's French lesson as follows:)

aigle
conversation
printemps
dehors
entendre
tuyau
parler
premier
ouvert
pied
voyager
ferme
vite
casuel
vert
oreille
acheter
apporter
chien
secret
quelque
savant
sale
profond
liste
violon
citron

**5. Forget "A"**

(Another conspiratorial message.)

530 X2P75 P2X0 9X S88IX2T 84I 55055 N97K75N2X0 9X W88S 88 AXX D5X024P 84T 5 4PX 5 LXXA 88 N75B

**6. It's Also Golden**

dashing brainy also Aesop giant fact maestro haggle jail avenue aerie case menace aorta implant bashful aegis brand swat

(Clue: Why was Aesop listed?)

### 7. Hear No Evil

(Lines of advice from an eighteenth-century father to his over-sensitive son.)

Study, sir! Never defend a fool. Be a sober soul, stoical. Rule no deceit. Work hard. Yours,

### 8. The Key to Escape

The following is a real cipher, sent to Sir John Trevanion while he was imprisoned in Colcester Castle in England during the days of Cromwell. He deciphered the message and escaped. Could you have done the same? Sir John was in prison for only a short period before making his dash for freedom. How long would it have taken you?

Worthie Sir John:–Hope, that is ye best comport of ye afflictyd, cannot much, I fear me, help you now. That I wolde saye to you, is this only: if ever I may be able to requite that I do owe you, stand not upon asking of me. 'Tis not much I can do; but what I can do, bee verie sure I wille. I knowe that, if dethe comes, if ordinary men fear it, it frights not you, accounting it for a high honour, to have such a rewarde of your loyalty. Pray yet that you may be spared this soe bitter, cup. I fear not that you will grudge any sufferings; only if it bie submission you can turn them away, 'tis the part of a wise man. Tell me, an if you can, to do for you any things that you would have done. The general goes back on Wednesday. Restinge your servant to command. R. T.

# 10
# BACONIAN CIPHERS

"It's hardly fair," muttered Hugh, "to give us such a jumble as this to work out."

*A Tangled Tale*

This cipher is named after its inventor, Sir Francis Bacon, the English philosopher and statesman. Bacon was greatly interested in cryptology.

Some authors say Bacon invented the cipher so he could write notes on his scientific discoveries and keep them secret.

In the form Bacon suggested, the cipher is intended for letterpress printing. The printer must use two slightly different type faces, but not so different as to be noticeable to the casual reader. Today, the Baconian cipher uses any two components. This will be explained in a moment. First, note the table below.

| | | | |
|---|---|---|---|
| A: | AAAAA | N: | ABBAA |
| B: | AAAAB | O: | ABBAB |
| C: | AAABA | P: | ABBBA |
| D: | AAABB | Q: | ABBBB |
| E: | AABAA | R: | BAAAA |
| F: | AABAB | S: | BAAAB |
| G: | AABBA | T: | BAABA |
| H: | AABBB | U-V: | BAABB |
| I-J: | ABAAA | W: | BABAA |
| K: | ABAAB | X: | BABAB |
| L: | ABABA | Y: | BABBA |
| M: | ABABB | Z: | BABBB |

Note that each A/B grouping of five letters is different. This cipher requires five symbols to represent one plaintext letter. To write the word BACON directly in this cipher, we would write:

```
AAAAB AAAAA AAABA ABBAB ABBAA
  B     A     C     O     N
```

However, that is not how Bacon devised it, that is, the message would not appear as A and B combinations. These combinations would be used, but would be hidden in an apparently legitimate message, using two not-quite-alike fonts of type to represent the A's and B's.

Although not as obvious as the following, it would work in this manner:

```
  B     A     C     O     N
AAAAB AAAAA AAABA ABBAB ABBAA
LOVEm AKEST HEWoR LdgOr OunDX
```

(A's are upper case; B's lower case.)

rewritten in normal fashion:

```
LOVE mAKES THE WoRLd gO rOunD X.
```

X = null

The Baconian can thus use any two slightly dissimilar components. You could fill a sheet of paper with dots and dashes—dots for A's, dashes for B's (or the other way around). Or use lower case and upper case letters, as above.

The Baconian Cipher lends itself admirably to photographic codes. One Christmas I sent a number of cryptogram friends a Baconian photograph of myself in my study. My books spelled out the message GREETINGS. I arranged them by groups of five, separated by book poles, and simply turned the books backward to represent B's, and left them in normal placement for A's. A surprising number of my friends failed to note the reversed books and thanked me for my picture!

While the Baconian is a rather clumsy cipher, it can be adapted to many interesting uses.

## PROBLEMS FOR SOLVING

### 1. Comment on the Baconian Cipher

BAABA AABBB ABAAA BAAAB AAABA ABAAA ABBBA AABBB

AABAA BAAAA ABAAA BAAAB ABBAA ABBAB BAABA AAABB

ABAAA AABAB AABAB ABAAA AAABA BAABB ABABA BAABA

**2. Secret and Urgent**

WE WilL DrIVe UP To sEE yOu NEXT WeeK on FriDAy anD

CAN STAy thE WEeKEnD. LOVe, JANe.

(The rule holds for groups of five.)

**3. Old Adage**

23574 34468 62488 42874 34898 67824 44256 42542

43279 66428 85623 42584 38847 21118 68368 78622

22389 66742 24896 92438.

**4. Carpenter's Rule**

IXAPR IOBEE AEIOU POOOX BAYFG MAYOE EAGOA TOAZI

YAFQP LOAIO OLEOA IOACY EESAA AOIEZ OEFAA EILOG

AHWOK POOIE OABEO AEIRA VOEZB DEOPA FYYSO OHEOE

EKQEA OOBME ATREQ ENNAO AEOCY OAMEA.

**5. You Call This Fun?**

NDCAZ HTUKP IOFWF SDCST ARBAL IZXMM CJPOB LLAUG

FTKBI LTONM CDXXN ABOFA ULLEG RHLBS CSCHM YEDAP

KLTIZ ZIAXQ FQXJJ.

(Is there another way of dividing the alphabet other than by vowels and consonants?)

**6. And Sometimes Never!**

P XX B CC QQ S TT L W O RR K A R T B Q Z A E W D G PP C F

TT O CC G H R KK V J MM L E A XX S A W AA LL B NN QQ E FF

G RR SS W E X CC KK O LL AA P S DD F V R EE JJ ZZ L M N T

O P GG AA XX F W PP FF PP C A B HH M Q S TT CC F R R G LL

T D GG H L OO TT C R AA B L QQ S N G D DD V OO NN C S E S

TT GG E O S N R PP H JJ ZZ E.

**7. What if it Pinches?**

a2 has my 3a7 2 he 4 age 466 we 7 up 2 hug 3 pa 323a

47a8a d3 deed 8a8a2 men 2 ex5 a3 ham 85 a7 feud 6

gophers 3 there 4 sun5 us 6a.

**8. Tried and True**

1 2 1 1 1 1 1 1 4 2 2 1 1 2 5 1 5 1 3 2 5 3 3 1 5 1 6 1 6 1

2 1 2 1 3 2 2 1 1.

(Clue: The above is a true Baconian, but with an added twist. It must be approached differently from previous Baconians. A first step is essential before actual decoding can begin. Study the numbers. How high do they go? Why? This Baconian eluded solving by an expert; if you crack it you deserve heartiest congratulations.)

# 11
# ADFGX CIPHERS

Clara [tried to] collect her thoughts. Her mind was a blank, and all human expression was rapidly fading out of her face.
A gloomy silence ensued.

*A Tangled Tale*

The ADFGX cipher was invented by a skilled German cryptographer during World War I. When enemy agents of Germany first ran across the new cipher, they were puzzled by the repetition of the letters ADFGX to the exclusion of all other letters of the alphabet.

In the original ADFGX cipher, there were three stages of encipherment, which made the cipher difficult to solve. For our playful purposes, however, we have stripped the steps down to just one.

Inside the alphabet square below is the alphabet, in vertical arrangement, with J missing (if a J is needed for the message, use I).

| | a | d | f | g | x |
|---|---|---|---|---|---|
| a | A | F | L | Q | V |
| d | B | G | M | R | W |
| f | C | H | N | S | X |
| g | D | I | O | T | Y |
| x | E | K | P | U | Z |

To encode a message, the encoder finds the letter he wants inside the square, then substitutes for that letter its coordinates outside the square, the first element always coming from the vertical row. Plaintext A thus becomes aa, plaintext F ad and so on, always reading from side to top.

The alphabet may be written into the square in a number of different ways—vertically as shown above, horizontally, diagonally, spirally, or with a keyword inside the square followed by the remainder of the alphabet. See Chapter 14 for examples.

To solve, using a tip which will be provided here for each problem, place the tip according to the pattern. Using the square above, the plaintext word "people" would appear as follows:

```
xf xa gf xf af xa
 P  E  O  P  L  E
```

Note how the P and E are duplicated in both cipher and plaintext. When you properly place the tip given, you'll be off to a flying start.

Guess at other plaintext words in the cipher, and try them out. Use the 5 x 5 blank square with the letters "adfgx" at side and top, and place letters within as you identify them. You'll discover that as you begin to recreate the alphabet square, you'll perceive the arrangement of the letters within it, which will help immensely with the solving. Ready?

## PROBLEMS FOR SOLVING

### 1. Driving Tip

aa da fg fg gg fg ff gg df ax ad gd aa dx ax dg gf xd

fg gd gg df gg xd fg dg ff gg df ax dd gd aa xa ax

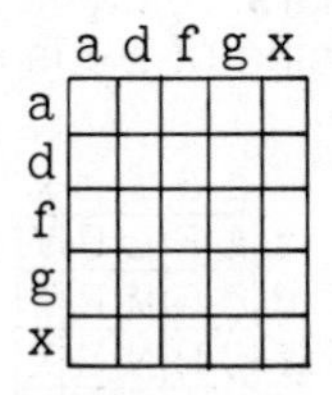


(Clues: The word FOOT appears in the plaintext. Look for a repeated digraph in the cipher.)

### 2. Don't Get Potted!

aa fa fg ad gf gd ax gg ff ax xa ax gg af fg fd ax gf

aa gf df fg gg ax xd dd gd df fg ga gd dg gg ax aa gd

gg dd gf da fg dx dg ax gd gd dd ff dg dd ff gd fg df

fg gd xd aa gd ax gg

| | a | d | f | g | x |
|---|---|---|---|---|---|
| a | | | | | |
| d | | | | | |
| f | | | | | |
| g | | | | | |
| x | | | | | |

(Clues: The word GETTING appears. In the ADFGX cipher, since any one digraph can represent only one plaintext letter, frequencies count. What digraphs appear most often? Could they represent plain E and T?)

**3. About This Cipher:**

aa ff gf gg fd xa dg ff aa df xa ad gf dg gg fd gd fg

fa gd xf fd xa dg gd fg gg fd xa fa fd xa fa xd xa dg

da gf aa dg ga

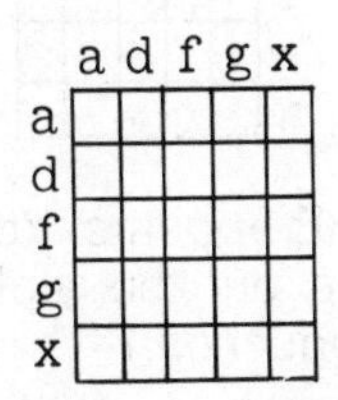


(Clues: Look for pattern word CHECKER. Have you noticed that there is no xx or ag in the cipher? Would that mean these represent infrequent letters such as Z and Q? Will that help you recreate the alphabet?)

**4. Call of the Wild**

ga df xf xa ax fd xx dd ax gx xx fd gg fx xx xf xf da

ag dd gg ax ff dx xf da xx ff dx dx df ff df gd xx gd

gd xx fx xg fg xd gf xx ff fd

| | a | d | f | g | x |
|---|---|---|---|---|---|
| a | | | | | |
| d | | | | | |
| f | | | | | |
| g | | | | | |
| x | | | | | |

(Clues: The word ATTACK appears. When you place the A in the alphabet square, you may perceive the arrangement of the alphabet in the square.)

**5. Secret of Success**

xf fg af xg xx df dg gx ax af ga dd xa ax dd gf gx ax

dd ax fa dd ax fa aa dd aa dg xx ga xa xd ax ax dg df

ga fa fa ga dd dg fg xa xx dg fd

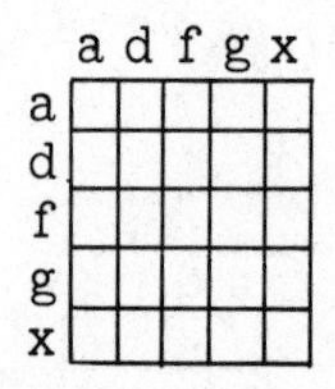

(Clues: The word WHERE appears. You may have some initial difficulty trying to figure out the alphabet placement in this cipher. Refer to the introduction.)

The foregoing ciphers were the elementary form of the ADFGX cipher, and perhaps the challenge is wearing thin for you. Okay, here's something different that will test your skill in anagramming (unscrambling letters to form words).

In the next problems, instead of using the letters ADFGX, five-letter words are used as keys for the side and top. To figure out what these words are, jot down the initial letters found in the digraphs and form these letters (there will be just five) into a word. Write that word down the outer left side of the alphabet box. Then jot down the second letters found in the cipher digraphs and make another word for the outer top of the alphabet square. Proceed as usual.

### 6. Kahoutek, for Example

ME TP ES CE OC MC TE EC CE OC CP TP OA CA CP OC OC TP

EE CE CE TS TP EC ES TP OA MC EE TE MS MS MC TP CC CC

EC TP MA CE TS CA TE MC CE MC MP CS OC CP MS CS OC OC

MS CE MC TP MS CS OE ES TE OC CE EC CS TE MS

| | a | d | f | g | x |
|---|---|---|---|---|---|
| a | | | | | |
| d | | | | | |
| f | | | | | |
| g | | | | | |
| x | | | | | |

(Clues: The word LITTLE appears. The first letters are METCO and the second letters are EPASC.)

### 7. Cashless

EO EE PN PO EE NY PM PN SO EE PM EM DE EN PO NN DM SM

DY PN PM DN NN NY DM PO SO DM EM EM DY PO PN NO NY SO

DY PE DY EO EE SM DY DE EE PM PE DN PE DY DE NO PO DN

DM PE DE PN

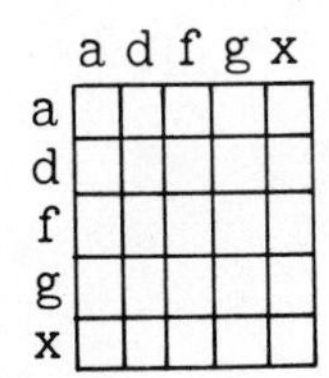

(Clue: The word WALLETS appears.)

### 8. Four-Legged Creatures

EE IE TO TS EH GS TE GE ES IH TE GR GR TO IO EE IE TO

TH TO TR TS TE TE IE EH TS ES TO EE GH IS TO TS TR TO

IH TE RH ES TO EH IR GH EE ES ES EE TS GH EO TO ES

| | a | d | f | g | x |
|---|---|---|---|---|---|
| a | | | | | |
| d | | | | | |
| f | | | | | |
| g | | | | | |
| x | | | | | |

(Clues: This cipher contains in the alphabet square a keyword followed by the remainder of the alphabet. The word CALLED appears.)

# 12
# COLUMNAR TRANSPOSITIONS

"There's a fallacy somewhere," he murmured drowsily, as he stretched his long legs upon the sofa, "I must think it over again."

*A Tangled Tale*

Would you assume that a cipher called a "columnar transposition" would involve transposing columns of letters? You would be right.

In this cipher, no cipher letters are substituted for plaintext letters. The original letters of the message are right there. But they are mixed up—not haphazardly, but according to a definite arrangement.

More complex variations of this otherwise simple cipher have been used by the French, Japanese and Soviet governments to send secret military messages.

To solve the columnar transposition ciphers in this chapter, you need only to put the letters in their proper order. Quite easy, but not as easy as it may sound.

Here is a quick look at how the cipher goes:

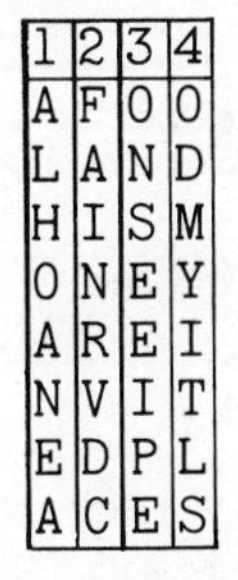

| 1 | 2 | 3 | 4 |
|---|---|---|---|
| A | F | O | O |
| L | A | N | D |
| H | I | S | M |
| O | N | E | Y |
| A | R | E | I |
| N | V | I | T |
| E | D | P | L |
| A | C | E | S |

The text reads A FOOL AND HIS MONEY ARE INVITED PLACES, written in a rectangle four letters across and eight letters down, in normal horizontal rows. But we "take off" the text *by columns*. We could do this in straightforward fashion by merely copying the vertical columns in 1234 order: ALHOA NEAFA INRVD

CONSE EIPEO DMYIT LS. (Grouping into five-letter sequences is customary with many ciphers, because it makes it easier to keep track of the letters and to recopy.)

An ally receiving this message would write it in columns of eight and then read it across.

However, we wish to make the message more secure. So we rearrange the vertical columns in some other sequence, not 1234. Perhaps we choose 2431, and our message then looks like this:

| 2 | 4 | 3 | 1 |
|---|---|---|---|
| F | O | O | A |
| A | D | N | L |
| I | M | S | H |
| N | Y | E | O |
| R | I | E | A |
| V | T | I | N |
| D | L | P | E |
| C | S | E | A |

If we take off the columns now, our cipher is even more secure from prying eyes. While the resulting code message is gibberish (FAINR VDCOD, etc.) we who know how it was encoded can easily unscramble it. We write the cipher vertically in columns of eight letters, then rearrange the columns in 1234 order and read across.

To solve the ciphers in this chapter: First count the number of letters in the cipher. Decide what format this fits into: 64 letters could be 8 x 8 (8 letters down, 8 across). 42 letters would be 6 x 7 or 7 x 6. We will not use rectangles here that are as disproportionate as 21 x 2.

Remember to copy the cipher in vertical columns. Next, rearrange the columns so the text makes sense reading horizontally.

Suppose your first two rows, after writing in columns, looks like this:

| H | R | E | P | T | I |
|---|---|---|---|---|---|
| E | O | O | F | C | I |

A little study will reveal the disarranged letters can be rearranged into

| T | H | E | P | R | I |
|---|---|---|---|---|---|
| C | E | O | F | O | I |

(the price of oi . . . oil?)

If you find you are unable to rearrange the letters so clear words appear, you may not have selected the right format. Try another.

## PROBLEMS FOR SOLVING

### 1. Silence is Golden

TLHHH ELBTW OWNAE OITIG NRPON ORNTS TTTUK EIFAT FI

(Clues: This cipher contains 42 letters. What number multiplied by what other number equals 42? Write the cipher vertically in the format you select. Then rearrange the columns. To help with the rearrangement—the first word in this message is BETTER. Of course you won't get that much help from now on. Use a separate piece of paper to try out your columnar arrangements.)

### 2. Maturity

MSCBS HLCUA TARAO GFOAD ECTAS EMRAN AOSCE YTNAE

TMUTS WRUOE UIFAE TOTLH TENR

(Clue: The word LEARN will appear when you have arranged the columns correctly.)

### 3. Don't Toot Your Own Horn

NSSRY NSTKA UROBI RNCUT OFRTO FBCPU FDTUO AOOYL

AAYLE YNHEW PGEH

(Clue: Look for plaintext word BACK.)

### 4. Me Jane!

FSIML GNFIS WEIYA SRRAU ERPEU EAYUT REOAP WLZER

CBNOR AIVOZ HNSTT RYATA LESO

(Clue: This one is just a bit tricky—check the title! The plaintext word EVER will appear.)

**5. We All Make Mistakes**

TOTAS ROHRI RSEEE FTETR HNYTR UMAGE CRWNY UICED

OHERA NLSPU ABGNM RRRVS ERTDE AOOIB AI

(Clue: The word ERROR is in the plaintext message.)

**6. Collectors' Item**

TARDA ITNEC ERGSW CRARO HKNLO CONND TNAUC ECOUL

OCROT LINYG UARPH LTSOO HFUIR NOTTE SIEPI OSIOF

(Clue: You'll find the word TROY somewhere in the plaintext.)

**7. Political Logic?**

WSCCC SRTTE TIWTR EACFK HHTHH YDROT OPAAU USGOR

CEILO RYORW MONIN IOELE ELSMT NHTOC OOIOE ITDNH

(Clue: Look for the word GET.)

**8. They Spit in Your Face Too**

LEARM ENOAC AWMSG STYUH OESHL RVIUA UUMAR IAYEO

SNSGE METSY ETXHL FDSAO AYAYA IATET LHAHR IETAO

RLMNV HUDNU HSSYR PETCN IGTEA EEMRE TAMNL HRHLU

(Clues: Can you solve this without help? If you need a clue, here's one: DEMAN ERA SLAMINA OWT.)

# 13
# NIHILIST TRANSPOSITIONS

For first you write a sentence
And then you chop it small,
Then mix the bits, and sort them out
Just as they chance to fall.

*Rhyme? and Reason?*

If you were to take the Columnar Transposition of the preceding chapter and carry the mixing process one step farther, you would have a Nihilist Transposition.

As with the Columnar, the Nihilist does not use substitute letters. The actual letters of the message are retained, but are mixed (transposed) in a certain order.

Suppose we wanted to make a Columnar Transposition from the text A PENNY SAVED IS A PENNY EARNED. That's 25 letters long, so we write it horizontally in a 5 x 5 square as below.

Step One

| | 1 | 2 | 3 | 4 | 5 |
|---|---|---|---|---|---|
| 1 | A | P | E | N | N |
| 2 | Y | S | A | V | E |
| 3 | D | I | S | A | P |
| 4 | E | N | N | Y | E |
| 5 | A | R | N | E | D |

Step Two

| | 3 | 2 | 4 | 5 | 1 |
|---|---|---|---|---|---|
| 1 | E | P | N | N | A |
| 2 | A | S | V | E | Y |
| 3 | S | I | A | P | D |
| 4 | N | N | Y | E | E |
| 5 | N | R | E | D | A |

Then we rearrange the columns—let's say in 32451 arrangement, as in Step Two above.

If we then took the text off vertically, we would have a Columnar Transposition cipher like those in the preceding chapter.

For the Nihilist, however, we rearrange the rows as well as the columns, using the same number arrangement, in this case 32451. This makes the cipher less penetrable.

Step Three

| | 3 | 2 | 4 | 5 | 1 |
|---|---|---|---|---|---|
| 3 | S | I | A | P | D |
| 2 | A | S | V | E | Y |
| 4 | N | N | Y | E | E |
| 5 | N | R | E | D | A |
| 1 | E | P | N | N | A |

The cipher is then taken off from the Step Three square vertically by columns: SANNE ISNRP AVYEN PEEDN DYEAA.

You can see that a Nihilist message must be written in a square, so that rows and columns may be shifted on an equal basis. This means the message must be 25 (5 x 5) or 36 (6 x 6) letters long, and so on. If a message does not fit into a square, nulls may be added (here, we use X). Or the message can be expanded or shortened by changing a word here and there.

To solve the Nihilist Transposition ciphers in this chapter, the above procedure is reversed.

Example: Cipher = RESME OAIYS TEVGF T.
With 16 letters, we know we have a 4 x 4 square.

First we write the cipher vertically into a square:

| | 1 | 2 | 3 | 4 |
|---|---|---|---|---|
| 1 | R | E | Y | V |
| 2 | E | O | S | G |
| 3 | S | A | T | F |
| 4 | M | I | E | T |

Next we try to anagram words in the rows, and may see VERY in the top row. Rearranging the columns:

| | 4 | 2 | 1 | 3 |
|---|---|---|---|---|
| 1 | V | E | R | Y |
| 2 | G | O | E | S |
| 3 | F | A | S | T |
| 4 | T | I | M | E |

Lastly, we switch the rows around in 4213 sequence:

| | 4 | 2 | 1 | 3 |
|---|---|---|---|---|
| 4 | T | I | M | E |
| 2 | G | O | E | S |
| 1 | V | E | R | Y |
| 3 | F | A | S | T |

Now off to your little black chamber,* lock the door and decipher these secret messages:

* The black chamber is a name given to secret decoding rooms operated by government intelligence offices.

## PROBLEMS FOR SOLVING

### 1. Gone Forever

SEITD ELAAH OLLSE TLOAD RASOR DSNES OSYRO T

(Clues: 36 letters make what size square? Copy the cipher vertically into this size square. Study the rows. Could Row 4 contain the scrambled word THAN? Do you see the scrambled word LOSE anywhere? Would that word fit with the title? Rearrange the columns, determine the correct number sequence, then shift the rows.)

### 2. Skirling Music

RNYXI ATERT EBSIE NPEUT AXSGN CVEIH INAMP T

(Clues: What musical instrument does the title suggest? Can you find this word out of order on one or two rows? Could Line 4 be the ending of a word followed by two null X's?)

### 3. Hard Won

EDIIE OYNOE EDCUI AIQRY EEAAA XQTNC SFXUH RRTUI

TMATS RNAB

(Clues: What letter always follows Q? The Q word appears twice and is seven letters in length. X's = nulls.)

### 4. Budget Problem

AMIRS IEANA KPEED OCCHW EOEEU GSMTA FEHCN TKWLI

EDYEN YRAT

(Clues: After making your square, can you find a scrambled five-letter word in the top row? Or, try the fourth row—perhaps you can see a word here.)

### 5. When the Going Gets Tough, Remember:

PTEEC BSASA SSBLC KIUSS LLETN MTSEO AWSSG OOBEC

TRTUS IASPS NCAGU HEEOC TNNT

(Clues: The longer a Nihilist message is, the more difficult it is to unscramble. Here's your first 8 x 8. The fifth row as you have copied the cipher contains an eight-letter word. Check the title. What do you call something that causes tough going? The fourth row also provides a good word for unscrambling.)

### 6. Loggerheads

LILHY ETRRE EEVLT FARMA EAULN NSSUG EDCMF BEOAO

TTETM SSAWG ACRYR OOAEE SGLI

(Clues: Look for the word EGGS. Then consider that word in conjunction with the title.)

### 7. Imported

ISRSE EULCL SGRVT TESIU AOAEN HITHR YHEHN FINOE

DHANE TAUCS NYTPS NPRET MEHSI OEUER AINIF CTCYI R

(Clue: The name of this cipher appears on two rows.)

### 8. Open 10 to 5

IOINS YSKIL FSTAT DEIEO UATIF OAEOE OTSRT AFSMS

RTHSI NLCFH GNOTL WOEER NEMOU ORMHU FTDIA ASCDN

IIETC NPOTO CBFPK SIDCY

(Clue: This crypt is about a doctor's office hours. Can you take it from there?)

# 14
# ROUTE TRANSPOSITIONS

"In Science—in fact, in most things—it is usually best to begin at the beginning. In some things, of course, it's better to begin at the other end."

*Sylvie and Bruno Concluded*

The Route Transposition cipher is a plaintext message written in a certain form (route) and taken off by another route. There is no substitution of letters. The Route Transposition differs from the Columnar Transposition in that the message is not necessarily written horizontally nor taken off vertically.

To illustrate, note the following routes by which the nine-letter word DISCOVERY may be written in a 3 x 3 square (follow the spelling):

1. Horizontal

| D | I | S |
|---|---|---|
| C | O | V |
| E | R | Y |

2. Alternate Horizontal

| D | I | S |
|---|---|---|
| V | O | C |
| E | R | Y |

3. Vertical

| D | C | E |
|---|---|---|
| I | O | R |
| S | V | Y |

4. Alternate Vertical

| D | V | E |
|---|---|---|
| I | O | R |
| S | C | Y |

5. Spiral

| D | I | S |
|---|---|---|
| R | Y | C |
| E | V | O |

Each of these routes has a reversed counterpart, which you can easily figure out by noting that the counterpart of No. 1 is

| E | R | Y |
|---|---|---|
| C | O | V |
| D | I | S |

Now say the encoder writes the message DISCOVERY (initially) by the horizontal route (1). He "takes off" the letters by another route, say alternate verticals (4). This does not mean that he uses Table 4 as shown here—he uses the *route,* not the letters. To clarify, we show that route again in numbers:

4.
Alternate Vertical

| | | |
|---|---|---|
| 1 | 6 | 7 |
| 2 | 5 | 8 |
| 3 | 4 | 9 |

Follow the numbers to see the pathway. Using this route to take off what we wrote in route 1, our cipher would be DCERO ISVY.

If the procedure is not clear, take a short message, or your own name, write it in a rectangle by one of the routes (add nulls if it doesn't fill up the space evenly), take it off by another route, and you will understand the Route Transposition cipher.

Other routes such as diagonal are possible, but are not used here. The problems in this chapter are based on the five routes illustrated and their five reversed counterparts.

To solve Route Transpositions, count the letters in the cipher, decide what size rectangle is needed, try writing the cipher by one of the routes and reading it by another. Trial and error is necessary. Don't be dismayed by that: when the United States tried to break the Japanese naval code in 1942, a team of cryptanalysts worked shifts of 12 hours on the code. Your task is certainly easier than that!

## PROBLEMS FOR SOLVING

### 1. Cynic's Version of Old Axiom

TSTIN OHOVU EUFES RMOIU RARSA INGUL

(Clues: To start you off, we'll tell you this message was written vertically by route 3 and taken off horizontally by route 1. To solve, reverse this procedure: write the cipher horizontally, then read vertically. Five letters across.)

### 2. Don't Overdo!

TORIV DOHST NEAUE TAGFG ROINT OESNM TORIE EPTSO

SLMOH ALYF

(Clue: When written in proper format, the word THE will appear vertically.)

**3. Don't Put It Off**

TSSOR DOTTH EPFTW ENOEN LDOOS UDKDA EMRNO AINNN

ORTCY

(Clues: When properly copied, the word TODAY will appear in the bottom row. If you have trouble, review the routes possible.)

**4. Hearing Problem**

AGOOB SHTLI OEAON EGNON SSDFW NSTLH AYITI LDYHE

SEOLE NIWDO REAS

(Clue: The word DEAF will appear in the rectangle backwards.)

**5. Wedding Belles**

OTYBI DROUG WDSNI LPNOE SISES IMDEM AHEYE NTEMC

TRNUS SAAIT AOUON BTLLR RHWA

(Clues: Sometimes a solver will write out the cipher in the correct route but cannot read it because he hasn't tried reading it by the right route. If stuck, refer to the quote from *Sylvie and Bruno* at the head of the chapter.)

**6. A Roof Over Your Head**

THETR OUBLI TALWA YSETT OBUIL CWAHM EDIDO IHCAL

DTAST TUEUO WSTHS MRDUO YSAIS AECIW TDESU OHMAE R

(Clues: Note the beginning of the cipher. Does it tell you anything about the route?)

**7. Rest in Peace**

TIEGT INOSE WETTA PGTTN ASTOP EUNHR SRINH EEWEE

NUNRQ NIOMT OOGOU ONSIS TCUFO TCINI UFPET SHHGL

SOUME EEEWE EENNP VETAV DTQOA AKOYO XOUDR RGRWN

(Clues: This is not as formidable as it appears. When you have written it out correctly you will see the word NOSE in the first row and the word WET i the second row. However, these words do not appear in the message. Don't let that confuse you. Write it out and you'll see.)

**8. Old Measurement**

ICEDD NALGN EFODR AWSTA KENFR OMTHE RNTEM OTDNE

DECAL PNDER DTOON EINCH EIEHE DDNDW ASEQU ALNOG

NCARA EEHTF OELDT FOHAT THREE BARLE YIKYR UTNEC

HTNEE TRU

(Clue: Some of the words in the message are visible in the cipher above reading forward or backward.)

# APPENDIX

## FIRST AID FOR THE AILING SOLVER

# A BAG OF TRICKS FOR THE CRYPTOGRAM SOLVER

These tips and techniques will help you become expert at solving simple substitution cryptograms of the kind described in the first seven chapters of this book.

When stuck, refer to this chapter for help. After a while, the techniques will be so familiar to you that you won't need to consult this chapter at all!

**1.** Check for one-letter words. That word is A nine times out of ten. If A doesn't work, try I.

**2.** A three-letter word may be THE, especially if any of the following obtains: (a) it begins the cryptogram, (b) both first and last cipher letters are of high frequency in the crypt, (c) the same three-letter word appears more than once.

**3.** Memorize the first six letters of the frequency alphabet, E, T, A, O, N, I. Each of these letters will normally show up as a cipher letter several times. You won't know which letters are which, of course, but at least you will have narrowed down the choices. The complete frequency alphabet is:

E T A O N I S R H D L U F C M W P G Y B V K X J Q Z

Cipher letters appearing only once or twice will probably represent plaintext letters in the second half of the above alphabet.

When you are frustrated by a cryptogram, counting letters to ascertain the frequency of repetitions almost always helps.

Special note on frequency counts: If a quick mental count doesn't get you anywhere in your solving, try a written count—far more accurate. Write down the alphabet. Take the first cipher letter and count the number of times it appears. Write down the total over that letter in the cipher alphabet. Check off the letters in the cipher as you count them, with a dot or small checkmark or whatever. That way you can easily spot overlooked letters. If you doubt the sloppiness of a quick visual count, test yourself. How many E's are there in the following sentence? *The frequencies of some letters in English writing enables them to be quite readily identified.* Write down the number of E's you counted. Now go over it again marking the E's as you count. How many did you miss the first time? (Caesar solution: SGDQD ZQD RHWSDDM)

**4.** Look for pattern words. If you can place one, distribute the letters where they belong throughout the cipher. Then check your non-pattern word list to try to identify partly completed non-pattern words.

**5.** Study and compare short words. Remember that every two-letter word consists of a vowel and a consonant. Suppose a cipher has these words in it: PQ, QP. What two-letter word can be reversed? Not AN, which reverses to NA. But how about ON, which reverses to NO, or the other way around.

Or suppose the cryptogram contains the words XP, RX and PQXG. Notice the duplicated letters. If XP were plaintext BE, then RX would have to be__B__not likely. Run down the non-pattern word list to find good candidates.

**6.** Try to identify vowels. This is a two-step process. First the solver tries to identify cipher letters simply as vowels rather than consonants; next he tries to determine which vowel.

Vowel-spotting can be done in several ways. One way is to examine how many *different* letters adjoin a high-frequency cipher letter. Since there are only six vowels, and U and Y do not have high frequency, then the four more-used vowels *must* touch the 20 consonants more often than the consonants can touch different vowels.

High-frequency letters usually include the vowels, so counting frequencies as outlined earlier will help in trying to identify the vowels.

A third way to pick out which cipher letters are vowels is to examine any sequence of five or six letters. One of the letters must be a vowel, and quite probably two of them are.

By combining these three methods a solver can usually make some good guesses as to which cipher letters are vowels.

The second step, determining which vowel is which, can be accomplished by studying the placement of the letters, whether they are doubled (AA is unlikely, so is II, EE is very frequent as is OO), and by use of the other techniques described here.

**7.** Punctuation provides clues. Is there a comma within the sentence? Does a three-letter word follow the comma? It's probably BUT, AND or YET. If there is a word containing an apostrophe, the letter following the apostrophe is probably T or S, as in WON'T GO, MAN'S HOME. If two letters follow the apostrophe, they are probably LL. If the cryptogram ends with a question mark, the first word is probably an interrogative like DID, WHO or WHY.

**8.** Look for reversed digraphs as parts of words, as in cipher words LBJMXB and BXQF, where XB and BX appear. These two cipher words represent plaintext WRITER and READ. The digraph seen most frequently reversed is in fact this one, ER. Others: TI, ES, EN, OR, ET, AT, ED, OF, AR, TO, AN, ST, ON, IR, IN.

**9.** Look for doubled letters. Letters that most often double are L, E, S, O, T as in WILL, SPEED, MISS, TOOL, ATTACK. Less frequent are F, R, N, P, C, M, G.

**10.** Repeated digraphs also help in solving. Some two-letter combinations appear more often than others. You would not see BX together even once in any ordinary cryptogram. But TH is frequently seen, as in the words THE, WITH, EARTH, THEY, THANKSGIVING, EITHER. If a crypt contains a digraph repeated more than once, try TH first. Others: HE, ER, IN, AN, ON, RE, AT, ED, ST, ND, ES.

**11.** Check the final letters of the cipher words. A letter that ends at least one word, and also appears with high frequency, may be an E or a T. A letter that appears only one to three times and always at the end may be Y. Letters which often appear as final letters include E, S, T, D, N, R, G, K, Y.

**12.** Word endings can sometimes be guessed if a crypt is partly completed. A word with an I third from the end may end in ING or ION. Besides these two very common word endings, others that frequently appear are ER, ED, ES, LY.

Finally, accept that no cryptogram obediently hews to all of these norms. E may be the most frequent letter in eight cryptograms out of ten, but in the others some other letter (usually a vowel) may appear most often. A crypt may begin with a three-letter word and that word may be FOR instead of THE. The average cryptogram, however, has enough conformities to permit solving.

# THE 1,000 MOST COMMON ENGLISH WORDS

The following pages list approximately 1,000 of the most common English words. The source is the *Word Frequency Dictionary* compiled by Helen S. Eaton (Dover, 1961, now out of print), which contains frequency lists for English, French, German and Spanish. I have made some subjective revisions to the list based on my own experience with cryptogram solving.

The words are divided into two groups, pattern words and non-pattern words. Plurals are generally not listed, nor are past tenses—SEEM appears, but not SEEMS or SEEMED.

Asterisked words are those which are not legitimately among the 1,000 most frequent words, but have been offered as clues in the cipher chapters.

For the solving of ordinary cryptograms (by "ordinary" I mean cryptograms not devised on purpose to be difficult) a short list like the following is more helpful than a very long list. With a comprehensive list, the solver must wade through dozens of rarely used words to try to locate the one he wants.

To illustrate, here are four texts taken from my *Games* page from an issue picked at random, along with an analysis of pattern and non-pattern words in the crypt and in the list.

**1.** Shakespeare said that all the world is a stage and we are all players. Unfortunately, most of us need more rehearsals.

This text contains 21 words (of which all but five can be found in the lists), three pattern words: THAT, ALL and NEED, and 12 non-pattern words: SAID, THE, WORLD, IS, A, AND, WE, ARE, MOST, OF, US and MORE.

**2.** A committee consists of several people who cannot do a job in several hours as efficiently as one person could do in one hour.

Total words: 24. Of these, 13, or more than half, appear in the lists, including pattern words SEVERAL, PEOPLE and CANNOT.

**3.** There are no unmixed blessings. Example: When a company puts in a four-day week, the employees lose two coffee breaks.

Total words: 20. Pattern words THERE and WEEK can be found in the lists, along with many non-pattern words.

**4.** Every taxpayer is anxious to know where his tax money is going and even more anxious to know where it is coming from.

Total words: 23. Included are pattern words EVERY, WHERE, GOING and EVEN and a number of non-pattern words.

Instructions for using the lists are included.

## HOW TO USE PATTERN WORDS

Ordinarily, if a cryptogram contains pattern words, the solver looks these up first, before trying non-pattern words.

Pattern words are words containing repeated letters. A few pattern words crop up so often in crypts that experienced solvers recognize them on sight. They include the words THAT, LITTLE, PEOPLE, WHICH, ALL and TOO.

Pattern words are very helpful, obviously. Once a pattern word has been identified, the solver gains a number of letters throughout the crypt right off.

To use a pattern word list, first number the letters in the cipher word you want to look up. Number the first letter 1, the second letter, if different, 2 and so on. When a letter is repeated, it takes the original number. DWW would be 122. WDW would be 121.

Then find that category by word length and number pattern in the lists.

To identify the right word in the list, when the list contains several words of one pattern, first check letter frequencies. Suppose you are looking up PWW and you note that the crypt contains a great many W's. Then the word is probably not EGG or OFF, since neither G nor F is normally a high-frequency letter. If the first letter of PWW is also of high frequency, you would rule out BEE for the same reason—B is not a high-frequency letter.

You can also identify the correct word by comparing words. If you have a two-letter word in the crypt, PW, and also PWW, then PWW cannot be ALL, EGG, ILL or SEE. Or suppose you have a four-letter word WXPW, along with PWW. Then PWW cannot be ALL—it doesn't work out with WXPW—but it could be ADD, making the other word possibly DEAD.

A little practice will show you that pattern words can be a dandy solving aid.

## PATTERN WORDS

121
DID
EYE

122
ADD
ALL
BEE
EGG
ILL
OFF
SEE
TOO

1213
AWAY
BABY
EVEN
EVER
NINE
NONE

1221
NOON

1223
BEEN
BOOK
COOK
COOL
DEEP
DOOR
FEED
FEEL
FEET
FOOD
FOOL*
FOOT
GOOD
KEEP
LOOK
MEET
MOON
NEED
POOR
ROOF
ROOM
SEED
SEEK
SEEM
SEEN
SOON
TOOK
WEEK
WOOD

1231
DEAD
ELSE
HIGH
THAT

1232
HERE
WERE

1233
BALL
BELL
BILL
CALL
FALL
FELL
FILL
FREE
FULL
HALL
HILL
KILL
KISS
KNEE
LESS
LOSS
MILL
MISS
PASS
PULL
ROLL
SELL
TALL
TELL
TILL
TREE
WALL
WELL
WILL

12134
ENEMY
EVERY
PAPER
USUAL

12234
ALLOW
APPLE
OFFER

12314
CATCH
CLOCK
ENTER
TASTE
TRUTH

12324
COLOR
HONOR
NEVER
SEVEN
STATE
VISIT

12334
BLOOD
BROOK
CARRY
FLOOR
GREEN
HAPPY
HURRY
QUEEN
SHEEP
SLEEP
STOOD
SWEET
WHEEL

12341
GOING
RIVER
TRUST

12342
KNOWN
LEAVE
ORDER
PEACE
SEIZE
SERVE
START
WHICH

12343
PIECE
THERE
THESE
WHERE

12344
BLESS
CLASS
CROSS
DRESS
GLASS
GRASS
GUESS
PRESS
SHALL
SMALL
STILL
THREE

121324
MEMBER

121345
MOMENT
SISTER

122314
APPEAR

**122345**
ACCEPT
ARRIVE
ATTEND
OFFICE

**123142**
INDIAN
PEOPLE
PROPER

**123145**
AFRAID
ALWAYS
CIRCLE
EXCEPT
EXPECT
EXTEND
SEASON

**123214**
DIVIDE

**123245**
FINISH

**123314**
LITTLE

**123324**
BETTER
BOTTOM
COMMON
FOLLOW
LETTER

**123342**
SETTLE

**123345**
BATTLE
BUTTER
CANNOT
CHOOSE
DINNER
FELLOW
HAPPEN
LESSON
MANNER
MATTER
MIDDLE
NARROW
SPEECH*
SUDDEN
SUFFER
SUMMER
SUPPLY
VALLEY
YELLOW

**123412**
CHURCH

**123415**
CHANCE
EITHER
HEIGHT
REPORT
RETURN
TWENTY

**123425**
CENTER
DOCTOR
HEAVEN
WITHIN

**123435**
SPIRIT

**123442**
STREET

**123443**
INDEED

**123445**
PRETTY
SCHOOL

**123451**
DEMAND
ENTIRE
ESCAPE
NATION
WINDOW

**123452**
BECOME
BEFORE
BESIDE
DECIDE
DESIRE
GENTLE
THOUGH

**123453**
CORNER
FARMER
FORMER
PLEASE
TWELVE

**123455**
ACROSS

**1213435**
EVENING

**1213456**
AGAINST

**1223456**
ACCOUNT
FEELING
OFFICER

**1231423**
PREPARE

**1231426**
INDIANS*

**1231456**
PURPOSE

**1232415**
DEPENDS

**1232452**
RECEIVE

**1232456**
GENERAL
SEVERAL
STATION

**1233245**
LETTERS*

**1233415**
SUPPOSE

**1233456**
COMMAND
FREEDOM*
VILLAGE

**1234155**
EXPRESS

**1234225**
BETWEEN

**1234235**
WHETHER

**1234252**
BELIEVE

**1234256**
CAPTAIN
HERSELF
PERFECT

**1234356**
PRESENT

**1234512**
REQUIRE

1234516
PERHAPS

1234521
THOUGHT

1234526
NATURAL
NEITHER
TEACHER
WEATHER

1234536
FORWARD

1234546
HOWEVER
MORNING

1234562
BECAUSE
MEASURE
SERVICE
THROUGH

1234563
CONTAIN
WITHOUT

1234564
HUNDRED
QUARTER

12134561
EXERCISE

12323421
REMEMBER

12324425
TOMORROW

12334567
POSSIBLE

12341546
TOGETHER

12343516
SURPRISE

12345367
BUILDING
CONTINUE

12345462
SEPARATE

12345463
INTEREST

12345467
PLEASANT

12345617
AMERICAN

12345627
ANYTHING
STRENGTH

12345633
BUSINESS

12345634
SOMETIME

12345647
PRACTICE

12345672
STRAIGHT

12345673
PLEASURE

12345674
ALTHOUGH
MOUNTAIN

12345675
INCREASE

12345676
COMPLETE

123244567
NECESSARY

123324567
FOLLOWING

123345467
DIFFERENT

123425671
YESTERDAY

123431564
CHARACTER

123435643
THEREFORE

123452673
GENTLEMAN

123456278
DIRECTION

123456478
BREAKFAST

123456523
CONDITION

123456776
AFTERNOON

123456785
CHRISTMAS

123456786
IMPORTANT

## HOW TO USE NON-PATTERN WORDS

Non-pattern words contain no repeated letters. They are also useful in crypt solving, especially two-letter and three-letter words.

Techniques are similar to those for pattern words. Suppose you see in a cryptogram a three-letter word TQB and a two-letter word QB. Checking your non-pattern word lists, you find such possibilities as AGO-GO and EAT-AT, while quickly ruling out ACT-CT and AGE-GE.

Suppose you have CWP and a longer word CPRAW. It isn't likely that CWP is AGE, for then CPRAW would be AE __ __ G. Learning to compare words in this way is essential to becoming a skilled solver.

## NON-PATTERN WORDS

A
I
O

AM
AN
AS
AT
BE
BY
DO
GO
HE
IF
IN
IS
IT
ME
MR
MY
NO
OF
OH
ON
OR
SO
TO
UP
US
WE

ACT
AGE
AGO
AIR
AND
ANY
ARE
ARM
ART
ASK
BAD
BAG
BAY
BED
BIG
BIT
BOW
BOX
BOY
BUT
BUY
CAN
CAP
CAR
CRY
CUP
CUT
DAY
DIE
DOG
DRY
EAR
EAT
END
FAR
FAT
FEW
FIT
FIX
FLY
FOR
GET
GOD
GOT
HAD
HAS
HAT
HER
HIM
HIS
HOT
HOW
ICE
ITS
JOY
LAW
LAY
LED
LEG
LET
LIE
LIP
LOT
LOW
MAN
MAY
MEN
MET
MRS
NEW
NOR
NOT
NOW
OLD
ONE
OUR
OUT
OWN
PAY
PEN
PUT
RAN
RED
ROW
RUN
SAD
SAT
SAW
SAY
SEA
SET
SHE
SIR
SIT
SIX
SKY
SON
SUN
TEN
THE
TIE
TOP
TRY
TWO
USE
WAR
WAS
WAY
WHO
WHY
WIN
YES
YET
YOU

ABLE
ALSO
ARMY
BACK
BAND
BANK
BEAR
BEAT
BEST
BIRD
BLOW
BLUE
BOAT
BODY
BONE
BORN
BOTH
BURN
BUSY
CAKE
CAME
CARE
CASE
CENT
CITY
COAT
COLD
COME
CORN

COST
DARE
DARK
DATE
DEAL
DEAR
DOES
DONE
DOWN
DRAW
DROP
DUST
DUTY
EACH
EAST
EASY
FACE
FACT
FAIR
FARM
FAST
FEAR
FELT
FIND
FINE
FIRE
FIRM
FISH
FIVE
FLOW
FORM
FOUR
FROM
GAIN
GAME
GATE
GAVE
GIFT
GIRL
GIVE
GLAD
GOLD
GONE
GRAY
GREW
GROW
HAIR
HALF
HAND
HANG
HARD
HAVE
HEAD
HEAR
HEAT
HELD
HELP
HIDE
HOLD
HOLE
HOME
HOPE
HOUR
HUNT
HURT
INCH
INTO
IRON
JOIN
JUST
KEPT
KIND
KING
KNEW
KNOW
LADY
LAID
LAKE
LAND
LAST
LATE
LEAD
LEFT
LIFE
LIFT
LIKE
LINE
LION
LIST
LIVE
LOAD
LONG
LORD
LOSE
LOST
LOUD
LOVE
MADE
MAKE
MANY
MARK
MEAN
MEAT
MILE
MILK
MIND
MINE
MORE
MOST
MOVE
MUCH
MUST
NAME
NEAR
NECK
NEST
NEXT
NICE
NOSE
NOTE
ONCE
ONLY
OPEN
OVER
PAGE
PAIN
PAIR
PART
PAST
PATH
PICK
PLAN
PLAY
POST
PURE
RACE
RAIN
READ
REAL
REST
RICH
RIDE
RING
RISE
ROAD
ROCK
ROSE
RULE
RUSH
SAFE
SAID
SAIL
SALT
SAME
SAND
SAVE
SEAT
SELF
SEND
SENT
SHIP
SHOE
SHOP
SHOW
SHUT
SICK
SIDE
SIGN
SILK
SING
SIZE
SKIN
SLOW
SNOW
SOFT
SOIL
SOLD
SOME
SONG
SORT
SOUL
SPOT
STAR
STAY
STEP
STOP
SUCH
SUIT
SURE
TAIL
TAKE
TALK
TEAR
THAN
THEM
THEN
THEY
THIN
THIS
THUS
TIME
TIRE
TOLD
TOWN
TRIP
TRUE
TURN
UPON
VERY
VIEW
WAIT
WALK
WANT
WARM
WASH
WAVE
WEAK
WEAR
WENT
WEST
WHAT
WHEN
WHOM
WIDE
WIFE
WILD
WIND
WING
WISE
WISH
WITH
WORD
WORK
YARD
YEAR
YOUR

ABOUT
ABOVE
AFTER
ALONE
ALONG
AMONG
BEAST
BEGAN
BEGIN
BEING
BLACK
BLIND
BOARD
BRAVE
BREAD
BREAK
BRING
BROAD
BROWN
BUILD

BUILT
CAUSE
CHAIN
CHAIR
CHIEF
CHILD
CLEAN
CLEAR
CLOSE
CLOTH
CLOUD
COAST
COULD
COUNT
COURT
COVER
CRIED
CROWD
CROWN
DANCE
DEATH
DOUBT
DREAM
DRINK
DRIVE
EARLY
EARTH
EIGHT
ENJOY
EQUAL
FAVOR
FIELD
FIGHT
FIRST
FORCE
FORTH
FOUND
FRESH
FRONT
FRUIT
GIVEN
GRACE
GRAIN

GRANT
GREAT
GUARD
GUIDE
HEARD
HEART
HEAVY
HORSE
HOUSE
JUDGE
LABOR
LARGE
LAUGH
LEARN
LEAST
LIGHT
LOWER
MARCH
MIGHT
MONEY
MONTH
MOUNT
MOUTH
MUSIC
NIGHT
NORTH
OCEAN
OFTEN
OTHER
OUGHT
PAINT
PARTY
PLACE
PLAIN
PLANT
POINT
POUND
POWER
PRICE
PROUD
PROVE
QUICK
QUIET

QUITE
RAISE
RAPID
REACH
READY
REPLY
RIGHT
ROUND
SHADE
SHAKE
SHAPE
SHINE
SHORE
SHORT
SHOUT
SIGHT
SINCE
SMILE
SMOKE
SOUND
SOUTH
SPACE
SPEAK
SPEND
SPOKE
STAND
STICK
STOCK
STONE
STORE
STORM
STORY
STUDY
SUGAR
TABLE
TEACH
THEIR
THICK
THING
THINK
THIRD
THOSE
THROW

TODAY
TOUCH
TRADE
TRAIN
UNCLE
UNDER
UNITE
UNTIL
VALUE
VOICE
WASTE
WATCH
WATER
WHILE
WHITE
WHOLE
WHOSE
WOMAN
WORLD
WORTH
WOULD
WRITE
WRONG
YOUNG

ALMOST
AMOUNT
ANIMAL
ANSWER
AROUND
BASKET
BEAUTY
BEHIND
BELONG
BRANCH
BRIDGE
BRIGHT
BROKEN
CHANGE
CHARGE
CLOTHE
COMING

COURSE
DIRECT
DOUBLE
DURING
ENOUGH
FAMILY
FAMOUS
FATHER
FIGURE
FINGER
FLOWER
FOREST
FORGET
FOURTH
FRENCH
FRIEND
GARDEN
GATHER
GOLDEN
GROUND
HEALTH
ISLAND
LENGTH
LISTEN
MARKET
MASTER
MINUTE
MOTHER
MYSELF
NATURE
NOTICE
NUMBER
OBJECT
PERSON
PRINCE
PUBLIC
RATHER
REASON
REMAIN
SECOND
SHOULD
SILVER
SIMPLE

SINGLE
SPREAD
SPRING
SQUARE
STREAM
STRIKE
STRONG
TONGUE
TOWARD
TRAVEL
WEIGHT
WINTER
WONDER

ALREADY
ANOTHER
ARTICLE

BROTHER
BROUGHT
CAREFUL
CERTAIN
CLOTHES
COMPANY
COUNTRY
DELIGHT
DESTROY
ENGLISH
HIMSELF
HUSBAND
INSTEAD
JOURNEY
NOTHING
OUTSIDE
PICTURE
PROMISE

SOLDIER
STRANGE
SUBJECT
TROUBLE

CHILDREN
DAUGHTER
DISCOVER
DISTANCE
NEIGHBOR
QUESTION
SHOULDER
THOUSAND

BEAUTIFUL
SOMETHING
WONDERFUL

Words with Apostrophes

DON'T
CAN'T
WON'T
HAVEN'T
DOESN'T
COULDN'T
WOULDN'T

Others

FLIGHT*
STRING*
AMONGST*
OSTRICH*

# OTHER CIPHERS

The cryptograms and ciphers in this book illustrate only a few of the methods by which messages may be disguised.

Here's a quick look at some other ciphers.

## ORDINARY CRYPTOGRAMS

As described in Chapters 1 through 7, these may be encoded in various ways. In addition to those explained, both cipher and plaintext alphabet may be keyed, rather than just one or the other. Examples:

Keyed with the same word in both alphabets:

*Plain:* A B D F G H M E X I C O J K L N P Q R S T U V W Y Z
*Cipher:* K L N P Q R S T U V W Y Z M E X I C O A B D F G H J

Keyed with different words:

*Plain:* L M O Q S U V W X Y Z P A N T H E R B C D F G I J K
*Cipher:* B E F G H W I L D C A T J K M N O P Q R S U V X Y Z

Neither of these coding methods adds complexity to the solving. Since only simple substitution is involved, letter frequencies, positions of letters and patterns of words offer a solution just as easily with one coding method as with another.

The advantage of coding the alphabets is to make it easier for a fellow conspirator to decode a message and to add a challenge for that solver who is not privy to the key used to recover the key as well as to read the message.

## THE ADFGX CIPHER

A tougher-to-break variation of this cipher (which was demonstrated in Chapter 11) uses four keywords instead of two.

| | B | R | O | W | N |
|---|---|---|---|---|---|
| | **E** | **B** | **O** | **N** | **Y** |
| WB | Z | U | P | K | E |
| HL | Y | T | O | I | D |
| IA | X | S | N | H | C |
| TC | W | R | M | G | B |
| EK | V | Q | L | F | A |

In this arrangement, the plaintext letter C can be encoded in any of four ways: AN, IN, AY, IY. The word BANANA could be encoded using three different digraphs for A and two for N. When this double-keyed method is used, frequencies of letters are veiled, as are patterns of words.

## THE GRANDPRÉ

The Grandpré is another variation of the ADFGX, and a favorite of members of the American Cryptogram Association. In this cipher, an encoding square of 64 letters is used, consisting of eight eight-letter words as below.

| | 1 | 2 | 3 | 4 | 5 | 6 | 7 | 8 |
|---|---|---|---|---|---|---|---|---|
| 1 | S | P | H | E | R | O | I | D |
| 2 | T | R | A | N | Q | U | I | L |
| 3 | R | E | J | O | I | C | E | S |
| 4 | I | N | W | A | R | D | L | Y |
| 5 | C | R | U | C | I | F | I | X |
| 6 | K | A | N | G | A | R | O | O |
| 7 | E | M | B | L | A | Z | O | N |
| 8 | N | A | V | I | G | A | T | E |

In constructing a cipher with this type of base, it's essential that every letter used in the message to be coded does in fact appear in the checkerboard square. In ACA usage, the checkerboard must contain every letter of the alphabet whether or not all of them are used in the message. In actual practice this makes solving easier, since there is a limit to the number of eight-letter words containing Q or Z, for instance. It is not necessary to create vertical words with this cipher, although this has been done here with Column 1. To encode, use coordinate numbers: 11 = S, 28 = L and so on.

## THE INCOMPLETE COLUMNAR TRANSPOSITION

The "complete" columnar transposition as outlined in Chapter 12 is quite easy to solve.

```
S O M E
C O L U
M N S A
R E L O
N G E R
T H A N
O T H E
R S
```

More difficult is the "incomplete" version. In this cipher, the number of letters in the message do not completely fill up a rectangle. The solver cannot simply write the cipher in a regular rectangle and shift columns, because he doesn't know which columns are short. The method of encoding and taking off the cipher is the same as for the complete columnar.

## ROUTE TRANSPOSITION

```
A C F K P
B E I O T
D H N S W
G M R V Y
L Q U X Z
```

This cipher is discussed in Chapter 14. The diagonal route which may be used for encoding follows the pattern of the alphabet at left. Variations are possible.

## THE VIGENÈRE CIPHER

A table for the Caesar Cipher is shown in Chapter I. The same table is used for the Vigenère.

However, the Vigenère is a "multiple-substitution" cipher—more than one cipher alphabet is used for encoding, and coding is done by columns rather than by rows.

| F | R | E | E | D | O | M |
|---|---|---|---|---|---|---|
| M | E | E | T | M | E | W |
| I | T | H | Y | O | U | R |
| L | U | G | G | A | G | E |
| A | T | T | H | E | A | J |
| A | X | C | A | F | E | O |
| N | W | E | D | N | E | S |
| D | A | Y | N | O | O | N |

Suppose you wanted to send the message MEET ME WITH YOUR LUGGAGE AT THE AJAX CAFE ON WEDNESDAY NOON. You would choose a keyword (any word; here, FREEDOM is used). Write the message out horizontally under this keyword.

The keyword dictates which Caesar alphabet will be used for each column. You would encipher the first column with the first letter of the keyword, F; the second column with the second letter of the keyword, which is R, and so on. That is, you would use the F alphabet first, then the R alphabet.

The recipient of your message, who has been cued in advance that the keyword is FREEDOM, will use his Caesar table to quickly decipher the message.

Variations of the Vigenere include the Beaufort, Porta and the Mexican or Quagmire cipher.

## THE RAIL FENCE CIPHER

This cipher retains the actual letters of the message, but transposes them by writing the message in zigzag fashion and then "taking off" the cipher by rows:

```
N       S       T
  O   I   T   E   I   E   NOW IS THE TIME
    W       H       M
```

Above is a three-rail, or three-row, message. The encoder takes off the cipher top row first, NST, then the second row, OITEIE, and lastly the bottom row, WHM. Written in the customary block of five, the message would become NSTOI TEIEW HM.

Assuming agreement was reached with the conspirator beforehand as to the number of rails to be used, the recipient will chart out a zigzag route in accordance with the number of letters in the message, write out the message by rows and read by zigzag. Graph paper is useful for this type of cipher.

If the solver does not know the number of rails or rows, but does know it is a rail fence, then solution is by trial and error. Count the number of letters in the cipher, chart out a zigzag route in accordance for, say, five rails, copy the cipher by rows and see if cleartext emerges. If not, another rail length must be tried.

## THE TURNING GRILLE

This may sound like a barbecue accessory, but actually it's an interesting variation of cipher technique.

Suppose you want to send the message LOVE IS EVERYTHING. That's 16 letters, which suits the Grille method just fine. Grille messages must form squares of even numbers: 4 x 4, 6 x 6, 8 x 8, 10 x 10, and so on. Nulls may be used to complete the square.

To see how the Grille works, take a sheet of plain paper and cut it in half. On each half draw identical squares four inches by four inches. Divide these large squares into one-inch segments as shown in Fig. 1.

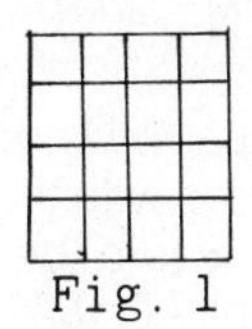

Fig. 1

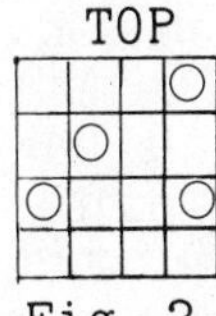


Fig. 2

Second, take one of the charts and cut out four of the one-inch squares as in Fig. 2, marking the top of the chart. Warning: The number of holes and their placement must be carefully planned. This detail won't be included here, but the reason will become obvious if you try your own messages.

Third, place the cut-out sheet exactly on top of the blank one, and write the first four letters of your message consecutively, as in Fig. 3.

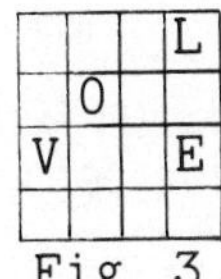


Fig. 3

Fig. 4

Leave the bottom sheet in place, but turn the cut-out sheet so that TOP is at right. Write the next four letters of the message through the holes. Turn again, so TOP is at the bottom, continue. The fourth turn will complete the task. Now just copy off the scrambled message from Fig. 4 and send it to your fellow conspirator. In five-letter groups, it would read HIILE OSRVN YETEG V. Your friend will copy the message in Grille form, place his identical grille over it and read.

## THE PLAYFAIR CIPHER

| A | F | L | Q | V |
|---|---|---|---|---|
| B | G | M | R | W |
| C | H | N | S | X |
| D | I | O | T | Y |
| E | K | P | U | Z |

This cipher is based on a 25-square alphabet. Above is such a square, with the alphabet written in descending verticals. Encoding is done within the square itself, two letters at a time, as follows: To send the message ARMY EMCAMPED NORTHEAST, divide the message into digraphs: AR MY EN CA MP ED NO RT HE AS TX (X = null).

Find the first pair of letters, AR, in the square. Using them as visual focus points, mentally compose a square with these letters as diagonal coordinates. Their opposites would be QB, and these become the cipher letters to represent AR. MY becomes cipher WO and so on.

Encoding problems will arise, which are solved as follows: If a digraph consists of doubled letters, an X is used to separate them. TELL would be TE, LX, L__and not TE LL. TELL LEADER would require another X, TE LX LX LE AD ER.

If the two letters fall in the same row, then use the letters to the right of each, recycling to the start of the row if necessary: For LV, using the alphabet square above, use QA.

If the two letters fall in the same column, use the letters directly below each, again recycling if necessary.

Ciphers akin to the Playfair include the Slidefair and the Seriated Playfair.

# EXPAND YOUR HORIZONS

The world of cryptology is an exciting one. This book has only opened the outer door to this mysterious world.

Herewith are listed an organization to join, books to read which provide a wealth of information on cryptology, and tools useful to the cryptanalyst, for those readers who are sufficiently intrigued to want to explore this fascinating realm more fully.

## AN ORGANIZATION TO JOIN

The American Cryptogram Association welcomes new members who are genuinely interested in the art. Write to Headquarters, Eugene and Evelyn Rogot, 9504 Forest Road, Bethesda, Maryland 20014 for information on how to join.

The ACA, at the time of this writing, had over 900 members, including some in foreign countries. Members adopt noms de plume (the author's is FLORDELIS) and address one another by these code names. Membership includes a magazine offering a variety of cryptograms and ciphers to be solved.

## BOOKS TO READ AND/OR STUDY

*The Codebreakers* by David Kahn (Macmillan, 1967). This book is the definitive work in print today on cryptology. It deals with the history of cryptography and cryptanalysis from early times on. It's also fun to read, with chapter after absorbing chapter on spies, rumrunners, presidential candidates, historical figures and romantic ladies all using cipher messages.

*Cryptanalysis: A study of ciphers and their solution,* by Helen Fouche Gaines (Dover reprint of the 1939 *Elementary Cryptanalysis,* 20097-3). Dover books may be ordered direct from the publisher: Dover Publications, Inc., 180 Varick Street, New York, New York 10014.

This book is used as a textbook by members of the ACA who want to learn more about ciphers. The author, code name PICCOLA, was a member of the ACA. She is now dead, but her book remains as the best and most complete text available today that explains in detail, one by one, the construction and solving of many types of cryptograms and ciphers.

*Cryptography: The Science of Secret Writing,* by Laurence Dwight Smith, is Dover reprint (20247-X) of the work published in 1943. It is written in simpler style than the preceding book, which perhaps makes it a better choice for novices. But it does not contain the wealth of detail that *Cryptanalysis* does.

Both *Cryptanalysis* and *Cryptography* offer problems to be solved, along with the answers.

*Secret Writing, An Introduction to Cryptograms, Ciphers and Codes,* by Henry Lysing (Dover, 23062-7, 1974). This is a simple exposition of elementary work in ciphering and deciphering. It is suitable for youngsters, but adults will also find it of interest.

*Codes and Ciphers,* by Frank Higenbottam. (English Universities Press, 1973, paperback, published in the United States by David McKay). This book, one of the "Teach Yourself" series, is fairly comprehensive and easy to understand. It offers both easy-to-follow instruction and good problems to be solved.

*Cryptogram Solving,* by M. E. Ohaver (1973, Etcetera Press, P.O. Drawer 27100, Columbus, Ohio 43227). This little booklet (32 pages) limits itself to the study of ordinary substitution cryptograms, such as those that appear in newspapers and magazines. It's the best of its kind in this field. Long out of print, it has only recently been made available again. Many charts and tables are included. The value of such a booklet is that anyone new to cryptogram solving who refers to this manual when stuck may soon find that he has painlessly absorbed enough information to solve many cryptograms quickly.

## A JOURNAL TO SUBSCRIBE TO

*Cryptologia* is published quarterly at Albion College, Albion, Michigan. This is a rather sophisticated magazine dealing with cryptology on an advanced level. Sample article titles: "Musical Cryptography"; "Data Compression Codes"; "Mathematical and Mechanical Methods in Cryptology"; "Analysis of the Hebern Cryptograph Using Isomorphs." For information about subscribing, write to *Cryptologia*, Albion College, Albion, Michigan 49224.

## A COURSE IN CRYPTOLOGY

Teachers who would like to offer a course in cryptology to their students will find a wealth of material available for them through the University of Oklahoma. Five teaching units or mini-courses are offered: Secret Ciphers, Solving Ciphers, Sophisticated Ciphers, Cryptarithms and Logic Unlocks Puzzles. Classroom quantities are low cost and a teacher's manual is included free. Books are geared to students five to 14 years of age.

The books are also available singly, or you may order all five with five instructors' manuals for $20. Write to Crypto-Project, Room 423, 601 Elm, Norman, Oklahoma 73019.

## CRYPTOLOGIC PUBLICATIONS

Aegean Park Press, P.O. Box 2837, Laguna Hills, California 92653 specializes in books dealing with cryptology. About 25 titles are currently available. Among them are reprints of former government intelligence publications, such as "Manual for the Solution of Military Ciphers" by Parker Hitt, published in 1916 by the Press of the Army Service Schools at Fort Leavenworth. Aegean will send a price list for available titles on request.

## WORD LISTS

Three word lists are currently available.

*Cryptodyct* (1976) by Eldridge and Thelma Goddard can be purchased for $4.50 from Box 441, Marion, Iowa 52302. This is a small paperback dictionary-type book containing both pattern and non-pattern words up to 14 letters in length. The book was put together from files compiled by the Goddards over a period of some years. Because it is a hand-compiled list (rather than done by computer) there are many omissions—words that ought to have been included but are not. Nevertheless it's a handy and compact reference and worth its small price.

*Pattern and Non-Pattern Words 2–6 Letters* (1977) by Raja is available for $9.75 from Raja Press, Box 2365, Norman, Oklahoma 73070. This is a collection of 24,000 words containing two to six letters, listed by word length and by pattern.

Additional volumes are planned for words over six letters in length.

*Pattern Word List* by Lynch sells for $14.60 from Aegean Park Press, P.O. Box 2837, Laguna Hills, California 92653. This book contains only pattern words (no non-pattern words) up to ten letters in length. Words are listed by pattern, not by length, so six-letter words may be mixed in with eight-letter words. (This does not pose any great problem, however.)

# SOLUTIONS

## CHAPTER 1, THE CAESAR CIPHER

**1.** Three-quarters of our population live in or near cities; the other quarter is on the turnpike looking for the exit.

**2.** Modesty is the practice of withholding from other people the high opinion you have of yourself.

**3.** Yesterday is a cancelled check; tomorrow is a promissory note; today is the only cash you have . . . so spend it wisely. Kay Lyons

**4.** The tomb of Tutankhamen, the Egyptian king, was discovered in nineteen twenty-two by an English archaeologist.

**5.** Borrowed brains have no value. (Consecutive alphabets are used, starting with A and progressing to end of sentence.)

**6.** Most anyone can direct you to happiness. It is midway between too much and too little. (Consecutive alphabets *by words*—each word begins with A alphabet.)

**7.** Many a short question is evaded by a long answer. (Starts with D alphabet, progresses to Z, starts over with A.)

**8.** Definition of a dime: A dollar with all the taxes taken out. (Keyword CHIDE.)

## CHAPTER 2, EASY CRYPTOGRAMS

**1.** Child to salesman at door: "The lady of the house isn't in. She's at her office running her company. I'll get the man of the house."

**2.** Always be tolerant of people who disagree with you. They have a right to their own ridiculous opinions.

**3.** Chinese proverb: He who asks a question is a fool for five minutes. He who does not ask a question remains a fool forever.

**4.** The big advantage of a credit card is that you don't know you are broke, at least not until the end of the month.

**5.** Today's children start kindergarten with an advantage. They already know two letters of the alphabet: TV.

**6.** "I know only two tunes: One of them is Yankee Doodle and the other isn't," Ulysses S. Grant once remarked.

**7.** Do you wonder where the younger generation is going? Safe bet: No place that can't be reached by car.

**8.** Greenland is the largest island in the world. Most of it is covered with ice thousands of feet deep.

## CHAPTER 3, CIPHER-KEYED CRYPTOGRAMS

**1.** (Key: BANQUET) Daniel in the lion's den: "Whoever has to make the after-dinner remarks, thank goodness it won't be me!"

**2.** (Key: INCOME TAX) If any more deductions are taken from our take-home pay, many of us will not have a home to take it to.

**3.** (Key: UNIVOCAL) Univocalic: Any writing using only one vowel throughout such as "Persevere, ye perfect men, ever keep the precepts ten."

**4.** (Key: PRUDENT) There are two kinds of intelligent people, those with enough wit to talk well and those with enough insight to be silent.

**5.** (Key: SKEPTICAL) An optimist may see a light where there is none, but why must the pessimist always run to blow it out? Michel de Saint-Pierre

**6.** (Key: MUSICAL) Did you hear about the church organist who took an extra job as janitor? Now he's busy minding his keys and pews.

**7.** (Key: OUCH) At no time is freedom of speech more precious than when a man hits his thumb with a hammer. Marshall Lumsden

**8.** (Key: OSTRACIZE) Lady at pet shop, "Is this dog pedigreed?" Dealer: "Yes, if he could talk he wouldn't speak to either of us."

## CHAPTER 4, PLAINTEXT-KEYED CRYPTOGRAMS

**1.** (Key: IDLER) If it required some effort to go from today to tomorrow, some people would always remain in yesterday.

**2.** (Key: JUDGMENT) Native Indians had the right idea. They managed to get rid of Manhattan before they had to pay taxes on it.

**3.** (Key: PUNISH) Revenge is a kind of wild justice, which the more a man's nature runs to, the more ought law to weed it out. Francis Bacon

**4.** (Key: TOADY) Do not offer a compliment and ask a favor at the same time. A compliment that is charged for is not valuable. Mark Twain

**5.** (Key: PAINFUL) Want ad: For sale, cheap, drop leaf table, leaves open to seat eight people, hinge holds them firmly in place.

**6.** (Key: REPUBLICAN) A Mugwump has been defined as a bird who sits with his mug on one side of the fence and his wump on the other.

**7.** (Key: WHODUNIT) Erle Stanley Gardner worked on as many as seven books at one time and wrote one hundred and forty novels during his lifetime.

**8.** (Key: PREDICTABLY) The town of Onoville, N.Y. was so named because each time a name was suggested at a council meeting, there was a chorus of "oh, no"s.

## CHAPTER 5, MISCELLANEOUS TYPES

**1.** A real friend is someone who takes a winter vacation on a sun-drenched beach and doesn't send a card. Farmers Almanac

**2.** Pessimistic remark: The milk of human kindness is sometimes skimmed, sometimes condensed, but most often evaporated.

**3.** A New York publisher brought out a volume of blank pages called "The Nothing Book" and was accused of plagiarism.

**4.** The Maldive Islands consist of thousands of lush coral atolls in the Indian Ocean. Many are uninhabited.

**5.** Anybody who finds himself going around in circles is probably cutting too many corners. (Written backwards—start at end.)

**6.** Know why Rip Van Winkle was able to sleep for twenty years? None of his neighbors had a stereo player. (Reverse each pair of letters.)

**7.** What we commonly call bravery is not the lack of fear, but its conquest. Sydney Harris. (Read alternate letters in sets of two—WHATWECO and so on.)

**8.** If you can spend a perfectly useless afternoon in a perfectly useless manner you have learned how to live. (Reverse the first two letters, then the next three in sequence.)

## CHAPTER 6, HARDER CRYPTOGRAMS

**1.** Those who should know say the ostrich does not bury its head in the sand to hide. But the myth is hard to dispel.

**2.** Credit for being wettest place on earth goes to Mount Waiaieale in Kauai, Hawaii, where heavy rains fall nearly every day. (Without the alphabet, you would probably have trouble with the Hawaiian place names.)

**3.** Thief walks around block, notes hock shop, comes back when dark, picks lock, quickly packs stock in knapsack.

**4.** A distinguished old prose-writing colonel once started to publish a jolonel, but quit . . . the expense was infolonel. (We warned you it was tricky.)

**5.** Man flew big box kite. Wind blew string around voltage wire, fire broke out, raged for hours, burned down homes.

**6.** Definition of "sponge": an expansible absorption module sensitive to differential molecular tensions.

**7.** Notice how often the young man who left home to set the world on fire had to come back to get more matches?

**8.** Windstruck nightfowl blown downstream, wingspread soaked. Bird alights amongst buckthorns, nightmare flight ends.

## CHAPTER 7, UNDIVIDED CRYPTOGRAMS

**1.** The rule in carving holds good as to criticism: Never cut with a knife what you can cut with a spoon. Axiom from Charles Buxton.

**2.** For some ninety percent of its existence, our planet seems to have had no ice at all at either the north or the south pole.

**3.** He who devotes sixteen hours a day to hard study may become as wise at sixty as he thought himself at twenty. From Mary Wilson Little.

**4.** Progress depends on individuals who are innovators, who reject convention and fashion their own worlds. Dr. Wayne Dyer

**5.** The tip of a lance borne by a charging knight in full armor had three times as much penetrating power as a modern high-powered bullet.

**6.** Four words that contain five vowels in alphabetical order are abstemious, abstentious, arsenious and facetious.

**7.** The trouble with some public speakers is that there is too much length to their speeches and not enough depth.

**8.** A good glass in the bishop's hostel in the devil's seat forty-one degrees and thirteen minutes northeast and by north main branch seventh limb east side shoot from the left eye of the death's head a bee-line from the tree through the shot fifty feet out.

## CHAPTER 8, KEY PHRASE CIPHERS

**1.** Do not give something up because you do not succeed immediately. Remember it may be the last key that opens the lock. (Little strokes fell great oaks.)

**2.** The chief advantage of speed reading is that it enables you to figure out the cloverleaf signs in time. (Sweet are the uses of adversity.)

**3.** Maturity is the age at which you begin to realize there are more things you don't know than you do. (There is no fool like an old fool.)

**4.** The good old days were the days when your greatest ambition was to earn the salary you cannot live on now. (Proverb: Better late than never.)

**5.** You see things, and you say "Why?" but I dream things that never were, and I say "Why not?" Bernard Shaw (Half a loaf is better than none. X=null.)

**6.** It is more from carelessness about truth than from intentional lying that there is so much falsehood in the world. By Samuel Johnson. (The truth has charm but it is shy.)

**7.** The Talmud says whoever gives a coin to a poor man has six blessings bestowed upon him, but he who speaks a kind word obtains eleven. (Kind words are better than alms.)

**8.** An irritable man has been compared to a hedgehog rolled up the wrong way and tormenting himself with his own prickles. (Anger can be a thorn in the heart.)

## CHAPTER 9, NULL CIPHERS

**1.** Waste not, want not. (First letter of each word.)

**2.** Come at once. (Third and last letters of each word.)

**3.** Dynamite bridge tonight. (Read third column down—first D in pudding, Y in fryer, etc.)

**4.** To solve ciphers, try everything. (Third letter of each word, but message reads upwards, starting with the T in CITRON.)

**5.** Opposition knows. Adopt Plan B. (Word divisions are meaningless. So are the numbers. Read every third letter in the crypt.)

**6.** Silence gives consent. (Read every letter that follows the letter A. Aesop, maestro, aerie, aorta and aegis might have given you a clue.)

**7.** Turn deaf ears to rude words. (Skip first letter, after that read 2, skip 4, read 2, skip 4 etc.)

**8.** Panel at east end of chapel slides. (Read every third letter after a punctuation mark. Did you miss the clue containing the words "period" and "dash"?)

## CHAPTER 10, BACONIAN CIPHERS

**1.** This cipher is not difficult.
**2.** Destroy papers. (Capital letters = A, lowercase letters = B.)
**3.** Practice makes perfect. (Even numbers = A, odd numbers = B.)
**4.** Measure thrice before cutting once. (Vowels = A, consonants = B.)
**5.** Solving ciphers is fun. (The first 13 letters of the alphabet are A, the last 13 are B.)
**6.** Miracles do not happen every day. (Single letters = A, doubled letters = B.)
**7.** If the shoe fits, wear it. (Letters = A, numbers = B.)
**8.** Old friends are best. (Numbers represent *how many times* a letter is repeated before it changes. That is, using A and B alternately, write each as many times as the digit indicates. Example: The word SPY in Baconian is BAAAB ABBBA BABBA. Starting at the beginning, B appears once (1), A appears next three times (3), then back to B for one appearance (1), next a single A (1), then three more B's (3), one A (1), two B's (2) and an A (1). Digits would then appear in a cipher as 1 3 1 1 3 1 1 1 2 1.)

## CHAPTER 11, ADFGX CIPHERS

**1.** A foot on the brake is worth two in the grave. (Alphabet square runs in straight horizontals.)
**2.** A lobster never comes ashore without great risk of getting into hot water. (Alternate horizontals.)
**3.** Another name for this cipher is the Checkerboard. (Straight verticals.)
**4.** Wolves are basically friendly and do not attack humans. (Alternating verticals beginning at bottom right.)
**5.** Luck is the corner where preparation meets opportunity. (Spiral.)
**6.** Comets are thought to be enormous balls of frozen gases with little solid material. (Keywords are COMET and SPACE. Spiral alphabet square beginning at *lower right.*)

**7.** Most of us wouldn't have such fat wallets if we removed our credit cards. (Keywords are SPEND and MONEY. Alternating horizontals beginning at lower left.)

**8.** The Romans called the zebra a horse-tiger because of its stripes. (Keywords TIGER and HORSE, alphabet keyword ZEBRA, straight horizontals.)

## CHAPTER 12, COLUMNAR TRANSPOSITIONS

**1.** Better to slip with foot than with tongue. Franklin (7 down, 6 across)

**2.** Most of us seem to accumulate birthdays faster than we can learn to act our age. (8 down, 8 across)

**3.** You cannot push yourself forward by patting yourself on the back. (9 down, 6 across)

**4.** If you cross a zebra with an apeman you will surely get Tarzan stripes forever. (8 down, 8 across)

**5.** Admitting error clears the score and proves you wiser than before. By Arthur Guiterman (9 down, 8 across)

**6.** The South African krugerrand is popular with coin collectors. It contains one troy ounce of gold. (10 down, 8 across)

**7.** How come those politicians who claim the country is ruined try so hard to get control of the wreck? (10 down, 8 across)

**8.** Llamas are very shy, yet have great curiosity and must examine anything unusual. Although of the same order as camels they are smaller with no hump. (12 down, 10 across)

## CHAPTER 13, NIHILIST TRANSPOSITIONS

**1.** To lose years is sadder than to lose dollars.

**2.** The bagpipe is a very ancient instrument. (X's = nulls)

**3.** It is easy to acquire an enemy but hard to acquire a friend.

**4.** At today's high prices we are lucky if we can make one end meet.

**5.** Obstacles are stumbling blocks that we can use as stepping stones to success.

**6.** Every summer giant female sea turtles crawl onto Florida beaches to lay eggs.

**7.** A group of Russian Nihilists in the late nineteenth century may have used this cipher for secrecy.

**8.** The most difficult task of the medical profession nowadays is to train patients to become sick during office hours only.

## CHAPTER 14, ROUTE TRANSPOSITIONS

**1.** To err is human, to forgive is unusual.

**2.** The one most important thing to save for old age is yourself. (Write by horizontals, 7 across, 7 down, read vertically.)

**3.** The kindness planned for tomorrow doesn't count today. (Write vertically, 9 down, 5 across, read by alternate horizontals.)

**4.** An old saying goes "There is nobody so deaf as he who will not listen." (Write in alternate verticals, 9 down by 6 across, read by alternate horizontals.)

**5.** A bachelor is a man whose mind is set surrounded by women all trying to upset it. (Write in reverse counterpart to Route 1, starting at *bottom left*, 8 across, 8 up, read in alternate verticals.)

**6.** The trouble with a dreamhouse is that it always costs twice as much to build as you dreamed it would. (Write horizontally, 9 x 9, read spirally.)

**7.** Novelist Ernest Hemingway wrote his own tongue-in-cheek gravestone epitaph quote pardon me for not getting up unquote. Of course it was not used. X=null. (Write horizontally, 10 across, 12 down, read in reverse alternate verticals starting at bottom right.)

**8.** In the fourteenth century King Edward of England decreed that three barleycorns taken from the middle of the ear and placed end to end was equal to one inch. (Write in alternate verticals, 16 down and 8 across, read spirally.)

# A CATALOGUE OF SELECTED DOVER BOOKS IN ALL FIELDS OF INTEREST

SECOND PIATIGORSKY CUP, edited by Isaac Kashdan. One of the greatest tournament books ever produced in the English language. All 90 games of the 1966 tournament, annotated by players, most annotated by both players. Features Petrosian, Spassky, Fischer, Larsen, six others. 228pp. 5⅜ x 8½. 23572-6 Pa. $3.50

ENCYCLOPEDIA OF CARD TRICKS, revised and edited by Jean Hugard. How to perform over 600 card tricks, devised by the world's greatest magicians: impromptus, spelling tricks, key cards, using special packs, much, much more. Additional chapter on card technique. 66 illustrations. 402pp. 5⅜ x 8½. (Available in U.S. only) 21252-1 Pa. $3.95

MAGIC: STAGE ILLUSIONS, SPECIAL EFFECTS AND TRICK PHOTOGRAPHY, Albert A. Hopkins, Henry R. Evans. One of the great classics; fullest, most authorative explanation of vanishing lady, levitations, scores of other great stage effects. Also small magic, automata, stunts. 446 illustrations. 556pp. 5⅜ x 8½. 23344-8 Pa. $6.95

THE SECRETS OF HOUDINI, J. C. Cannell. Classic study of Houdini's incredible magic, exposing closely-kept professional secrets and revealing, in general terms, the whole art of stage magic. 67 illustrations. 279pp. 5⅜ x 8½. 22913-0 Pa. $3.00

HOFFMANN'S MODERN MAGIC, Professor Hoffmann. One of the best, and best-known, magicians' manuals of the past century. Hundreds of tricks from card tricks and simple sleight of hand to elaborate illusions involving construction of complicated machinery. 332 illustrations. 563pp. 5⅜ x 8½. 23623-4 Pa. $6.00

MADAME PRUNIER'S FISH COOKERY BOOK, Mme. S. B. Prunier. More than 1000 recipes from world famous Prunier's of Paris and London, specially adapted here for American kitchen. Grilled tournedos with anchovy butter, Lobster a la Bordelaise, Prunier's prized desserts, more. Glossary. 340pp. 5⅜ x 8½. (Available in U.S. only) 22679-4 Pa. $3.00

FRENCH COUNTRY COOKING FOR AMERICANS, Louis Diat. 500 easy-to-make, authentic provincial recipes compiled by former head chef at New York's Fitz-Carlton Hotel: onion soup, lamb stew, potato pie, more. 309pp. 5⅜ x 8½. 23665-X Pa. $3.95

SAUCES, FRENCH AND FAMOUS, Louis Diat. Complete book gives over 200 specific recipes: bechamel, Bordelaise, hollandaise, Cumberland, apricot, etc. Author was one of this century's finest chefs, originator of vichyssoise and many other dishes. Index. 156pp. 5⅜ x 8. 23663-3 Pa. $2.50

TOLL HOUSE TRIED AND TRUE RECIPES, Ruth Graves Wakefield. Authentic recipes from the famous Mass. restaurant: popovers, veal and ham loaf, Toll House baked beans, chocolate cake crumb pudding, much more. Many helpful hints. Nearly 700 recipes. Index. 376pp. 5⅜ x 8½. 23560-2 Pa. $4.50

## *CATALOGUE OF DOVER BOOKS*

THE EARLY WORK OF AUBREY BEARDSLEY, Aubrey Beardsley. 157 plates, 2 in color: *Manon Lescaut, Madame Bovary, Morte Darthur, Salome,* other. Introduction by H. Marillier. 182pp. 8⅛ x 11. 21816-3 Pa. $4.50

THE LATER WORK OF AUBREY BEARDSLEY, Aubrey Beardsley. Exotic masterpieces of full maturity: *Venus and Tannhauser, Lysistrata, Rape of the Lock, Volpone,* Savoy material, etc. 174 plates, 2 in color. 186pp. 8⅛ x 11. 21817-1 Pa. $4.50

THOMAS NAST'S CHRISTMAS DRAWINGS, Thomas Nast. Almost all Christmas drawings by creator of image of Santa Claus as we know it, and one of America's foremost illustrators and political cartoonists. 66 illustrations. 3 illustrations in color on covers. 96pp. 8⅜ x 11¼.
23660-9 Pa. $3.50

THE DORÉ ILLUSTRATIONS FOR DANTE'S DIVINE COMEDY, Gustave Doré. All 135 plates from Inferno, Purgatory, Paradise; fantastic tortures, infernal landscapes, celestial wonders. Each plate with appropriate (translated) verses. 141pp. 9 x 12. 23231-X Pa. $4.50

DORÉ'S ILLUSTRATIONS FOR RABELAIS, Gustave Doré. 252 striking illustrations of *Gargantua and Pantagruel* books by foremost 19th-century illustrator. Including 60 plates, 192 delightful smaller illustrations. 153pp. 9 x 12. 23656-0 Pa. $5.00

LONDON: A PILGRIMAGE, Gustave Doré, Blanchard Jerrold. Squalor, riches, misery, beauty of mid-Victorian metropolis; 55 wonderful plates, 125 other illustrations, full social, cultural text by Jerrold. 191pp. of text. 9⅜ x 12¼. 22306-X Pa. $6.00

THE RIME OF THE ANCIENT MARINER, Gustave Doré, S. T. Coleridge. Dore's finest work, 34 plates capture moods, subtleties of poem. Full text. Introduction by Millicent Rose. 77pp. 9¼ x 12. 22305-1 Pa. $3.50

THE DORE BIBLE ILLUSTRATIONS, Gustave Doré. All wonderful, detailed plates: Adam and Eve, Flood, Babylon, Life of Jesus, etc. Brief King James text with each plate. Introduction by Millicent Rose. 241 plates. 241pp. 9 x 12. 23004-X Pa. $6.00

THE COMPLETE ENGRAVINGS, ETCHINGS AND DRYPOINTS OF ALBRECHT DURER. "Knight, Death and Devil"; "Melencolia," and more—all Dürer's known works in all three media, including 6 works formerly attributed to him. 120 plates. 235pp. 8⅜ x 11¼.
22851-7 Pa. $6.50

MAXIMILIAN'S TRIUMPHAL ARCH, Albrecht Dürer and others. Incredible monument of woodcut art: 8 foot high elaborate arch—heraldic figures, humans, battle scenes, fantastic elements—that you can assemble yourself. Printed on one side, layout for assembly. 143pp. 11 x 16.
21451-6 Pa. $5.00